DATE DUE

THE REFERENCE SHELF   VOLUME 41 NUMBER 5

COLLECTIVE BARGAINING FOR PUBLIC EMPLOYEES

EDITED BY

HERBERT L. MARX, JR.

THE H. W. WILSON COMPANY

NEW YORK   1969

THE REFERENCE SHELF

The books in this series contain reprints of articles, excerpts from books, and addresses on current issues and social trends in the United States and other countries. There are six separately bound numbers in each volume, all of which are generally published in the same calendar year. One number is a collection of recent speeches; each of the others is devoted to a single subject and gives background information and discussion from various points of view, concluding with a comprehensive bibliography.

Subscribers to the current volume receive the books as issued. The subscription rate is $14 in the United States and Canada ($17 foreign) for a volume of six numbers. Single numbers are $3.50 each in the United States and Canada ($4 foreign).

COLLECTIVE BARGAINING FOR PUBLIC EMPLOYEES

Copyright © 1969
By The H. W. Wilson Company

Standard Book Number 8242-0110-8

Library of Congress Catalog Card Number 69-15810

PRINTED IN THE UNITED STATES OF AMERICA

PREFACE

Is public sector unionism a brand new phenomenon, or is it simply an extension of the American trade union movement?

Certainly the sharpest distinction is that unions representing governmental employees are not dealing with a profit-oriented employer, who in economic contest is fair game. Government, at any level, is nonprofit, essential, and sovereign—at least in theory. But this may become a theoretical distinction, as the illegal, supposedly intolerable, strike against governmental bodies becomes almost openly accepted in many areas. Further, resolution of differences is more and more frequently referred to a third party for final and binding decision.

On this basis, the growing strength of unions in the public sector may be considered an extension, a development in a tangential direction, of the American trade union movement. In its historical context, as many observers have noted, the sequence follows this pattern: The decade of the 1930s, with the National Labor Relations (Wagner) Act of 1935, witnessed the early development of mass industrial unions. The 1940s, with World War II freezes on wages and prices and the Taft-Hartley Act amendments to the basic labor law in 1947, saw a stabilization of labor-management relations; growth in union power was offset by legal restrictions that favored management. The 1950s brought legal attention to the protection of the individual union member (and non-union employee) against so-called big unions and, in a few particular instances, corrupt union practices. In the decade of the 1960s, the simultaneous rise of government employment at all levels, Federal encouragement of collective bargaining by President John F. Kennedy, civil rights activism and civil disobedience in defiance of the legal pro-

3

hibition of strikes by government workers—all have contributed to the growing importance of collective bargaining for public employees.

New developments have brought new approaches to the subject, coupled with much rethinking of traditional attitudes toward government workers and their relationships with their employers. As in the general field of collective bargaining, there is no unanimity of thought, but at the start of the 1970s these three general conclusions predominate:

1. Government employees at all levels should have the right to organize and be represented in collective bargaining, in much the same manner as workers in the private sector.

2. Strikes by government employees—whether in essential or nonessential types of work—are fundamentally wrong and contrary to our theories of the sovereignty of the state, even though on a practical basis such strikes have been uneasily tolerated.

3. How to reconcile these two concepts remains the major labor-management perplexity of our time. As noted throughout this volume, governmental authorities at all levels, unions, and labor-management theorists are all wrestling with the problem. The suggested courses of action are not yet widely accepted, nor is there a resolution of the basic difficulty: preserving the right of collective bargaining short of the right to strike.

These uncertainties, this searching for answers by men of good will, are threads which run throughout the fabric of this book. Section I provides an overview of the situation today. Section II looks inside the workings of unions within the public employment field—some unions of long tenure now assuming new importance, others coming to the limelight for the first time.

Section III deals with all aspects of that phase of public unionism which has hit home most severely over the past few years—union activities in education. Are teachers simply employees entitled to the same representational rights as postal clerks? as auto workers? Or does their special role in society require an entirely different employee status? These are the questions reviewed in "Teachers and Collective Bargaining."

As alluded to above, the central problem is that of strikes of government employees. This is true not only for the same reasons that apply to work stoppages in private industry but also for a number of other reasons applying uniquely to governmental employees. Not the least of these reasons is the threat of public disorder and even the possibility of anarchy, as exemplified by the recent strike of police and firemen in Montreal. Section IV discusses these questions, and Section V, the legal aspects of governmental labor relations.

Section VI deals with public employment bargaining abroad; European nations, it can be seen, are more liberal in some cases and more restrictive in others. Finally, Section VII takes a look ahead. While specific predictions of future developments are hazardous, it seems safe to say that the spiraling importance of the relationship among government employees, governmental units, and the public requires intensive thought and decision if we are to bring stability into public sector collective bargaining.

The editor expresses sincere appreciation to the organizations, publications, and authors who have granted permission to include the materials that make up this volume. Special acknowledgment is also made to Paul G. Kell, arbitrator and labor-management consultant, who suggested many sources, and to Kenneth F. Kahn, a student at Harvard Law School, who assisted in portions of the research.

HERBERT L. MARX, JR.

October 1969

CONTENTS

V.   THE LAW

VI.   PUBLIC UNIONISM ABROAD

I. THE BACKGROUND OF PUBLIC SECTOR UNIONISM

EDITOR'S INTRODUCTION

In this preview section, three noted experts take a summary view of public sector unionism. In the field of public administration Frank P. Zeidler reviews the phenomenal growth in numbers and importance of this portion of the labor movement. Professor Everett M. Kassalow, who has written widely on the topic, examines the background and organizational makeup of public employee unions. Former Senator Wayne Morse, a leading expert in labor-management matters during his long career, pinpoints the effect of the "black revolution" as it impinges on public employment and labor-management relations.

PUBLIC SERVANTS AS ORGANIZED LABOR [1]

Just as employee-management relations in private industry were revolutionized some thirty years ago, employee-management relations in the public sector have recently been undergoing drastic changes. They are less spectacular, but they may be more fundamental, because they profoundly affect governmental procedure.

There are now twice as many local and state government employees as there were twenty years ago, and they represent about 10 per cent of all union members. One of the results is that the theory of sovereignty of public officials in municipal matters has been greatly modified; the home rule doctrine that municipalities used to rely on as a means of protecting

[1] From article by Frank P. Zeidler, umpire for American Federation of State, County and Municipal Employees, District 48 and Milwaukee County, public administration consultant, and former mayor of Milwaukee. *Personnel.* 46:44-7. Jl.-Ag. '69. Reprinted by permission of the publisher from *Personnel,* July/August 1969, © by the American Management Association, Inc.

themselves from state legislative acts no longer holds, or at least is being seriously threatened.

In several states, legislatures have ruled that conditions of employment in local government must be jointly determined by organized employees and elected public officials or their designated chief negotiating officers, and this sharing of powers in wage determination and conditions of employment through the negotiation process has in turn diminished public officials' authority in other areas of policy involving organized employees.

The net effect has been to create what amounts to a two-chamber local government. One chamber is made up of elected representatives and chief executives—aldermen, councilmen, county board or commission members, mayors or other chief executives—the traditional decision-making body for local government. The other chamber comprises the organized public employees who have gained official recognition to negotiate. The public business on wages and conditions of work, and therefore indirectly on policy, cannot be carried on without mutual agreement between these two chambers, much as the laws of Congress require the approval of both houses.

The implications of this new method of reaching decisions in local government put an entirely different aspect on the sovereignty of councils and executives and elected officials as well. The challenge of organized public employees can mean considerable loss of control over the budget, and hence over tax rates and over government programs and projects. The gravity of the challenge was recognized by some municipal officials at least ten years ago, but most of them took the position that to study the new phenomenon was to encourage it. As is usually the case, the ostrich stance was a mistake: When employee organizations suddenly burgeoned, municipal officials were not prepared with effective rejoinders before legislatures and in negotiations.

Meanwhile, organized public employees' methods of making demands, including the strike, have had considerable success. Without legislation, some organized public employees, such as firemen and construction workers, have been able to achieve informal but highly effective bargaining conditions with public officials. In many cases legislation merely trailed along to give official approval to current practice.

In organizing public service workers, a significant breakthrough came with the adoption of the industrial union concept, which quickly brought in mass numbers of members. The chief exponent of this approach is the American Federation of State, County and Municipal Employees [see "The AFGE and the AFSCME," in Section II, below], which has pooled its legislative strength with employees' unions in the private sector; it thus succeeded in organizing some cities and getting city recognition without formal legislation more than thirty years ago. In 1959, with the help of the other AFL-CIO unions, it won recognition for public employee organizations from the Wisconsin legislature—its first major state legislative success.

Every year since then, additional legislative gains have been made by public employee organizations in their quest for more power over the decisions that affect public employment. Now that the principle of compulsory arbitration has been widely accepted, giving employee organizations parity with employers, elected local officials can be subject to the decisions of an arbitrator, further evidence that in decisions affecting local conditions of employment they no longer have the last word.

In sum, it must now be clear that the sovereignty local municipal officials thought they had (but really did not have under state legislatures) is disappearing in many places in the United States, and even the sovereign rights state governments had under the powers residual with them under the Constitution are being diminished as state employees gain negotiating strength. This is a revolutionary principle rather quietly at work in American government.

Several conditions have favored the increased strength of government employees. In the first place, the substantial growth in public employment made inevitable the emergence of a public employee group consciousness that led to group organization. When many employees are working at the same kind of job, they are bound to draw together when friction between them and management arises; formal organization gives them a voice to express grievances and make demands.

Moreover, the growth of organized labor in the private sector of the economy has been reflected in growth of organizations in the public sector. Employee organizations in the public service are closely related to large cities and industrialized areas, where unions have succeeded in electing officials who are sympathetic to the views of labor and willing to support legislation recognizing and giving negotiating powers to organized public employees.

In addition, the civil service system, originally conceived to protect public employees from the spoils system, among some employees has tended to create hostility toward public administration. The merit principle of promotion and the hierarchical structure of governments necessarily create a pyramidal system for advancement, but of course not everyone can reach the top. Those who can't get anywhere near it seek other means of improving income and maintaining their self-respect, and employee organizations furnish both a method of challenging the rules of advancement under the merit system and a route toward higher income if advancement is stymied. On the other hand, when public employees organize, the civil service system provides shelter and protection against managerial reaction.

The increase in sheer numbers of public employees also may foster the employee's sense of being exploited. Employees' representatives often complain that public employees are second-class citizens and that public employers exploit employees just as private employers do. With this attitude, public employees, like those in private industry, turn to unions. Then it is a short step to making demands to end the exploitation. The final stage of such demands is the work stoppage.

A NEW KIND OF UNIONIST [2]

Strikes of public employees, once a novelty, are no longer unusual. During one three-month period, not so long ago, a casual check showed social workers' strikes in Chicago, Sacramento, and White Plains; slowdowns of firefighters in Buffalo and of policemen in Detroit; strikes among university maintenance employees at Ohio State, Indiana, and the University of Kansas Medical Center; a three-day "heal-in" by the interns and residents of the Boston City Hospital; "informational" picketing, with a strike threat, by the Philadelphia School Nurses' Association; teachers' strikes in a dozen communities, ranging from West Mifflin, Pennsylvania, and Gibraltor, Ohio, to South Bend, Indiana, and Baltimore, Maryland. Such strikes and slowdowns among teachers, policemen, firemen, etc. have become daily occurrences. Because there had been a growing feeling that industrial relations were becoming more "mature," strikes of this sort in sectors hitherto unidentified with unionism have led to confusion. Large-scale unionization of government workers is a relatively new phenomenon in this country, although it has been common in almost all other democratic industrial countries of the world. That large-scale public-employee unionism was also inevitable in the United States at some time is clear. But why now? What new forces account for the current upsurge of public unionism?

The first of these forces has been the institutionalization of trade unionism in American life. Unions date back more than one hundred fifty years in the United States. But large-scale unionism dates only from the late 1930s, and it has only been in the past decade or so that collective bargaining has become widely accepted as the appropriate way to settle wages

[2] From "Trade Unionism Goes Public," by Everett M. Kassalow, professor of economics, University of Wisconsin. *Public Interest*. p 118-22. Winter '69. © National affairs, Inc.—1969. Reprinted by permission.

and working issues. During this decade unionists have become respectable. Union leaders have been named to innumerable presidential commissions dealing with every conceivable problem area of the country's foreign and domestic business.

It is not surprising thus that, despite the revelations in the Senate investigations of the malfeasance of Jimmy Hoffa and a few other union leaders, public opinion surveys show that union officers have registered a significant gain in occupational prestige between 1947 and 1963. This gain is clearly attributable to the widespread acceptance of the basic value of unionism in society, and this legitimacy is being transferred to public employees as well. For this reason, unionism among government workers has begun to advance rapidly, and there is every prospect it will continue to grow.

There is a second, more specific reason for the recent growth of government unionism, and this is Executive Order 10988 [see "Executive Order 10988," in Section V, below] issued by President John F. Kennedy in January 1962, which encouraged unionism in the Federal service. In its support of public unionism, this order was as clear and unequivocal as the Wagner Act of 1935 had been in its support for unions and collective bargaining in the private sector. It declared that "the efficient administration of the government and the well-being of employees require that orderly and constructive relationships be maintained between employee organizations and management."

In New York City, earlier orders issued by Mayor Robert Wagner resulted in the "breakthrough" of unionism in 1961 among 44,000 teachers. Kennedy's order has a spillover effect in legitimating unionism in states and local public service. Further, the reapportionment of state legislatures seems to have had a generally liberalizing effect, and a flow of new legislation in a dozen states has expedited public employee bargaining.

The enormous growth in public employment has also acted to transform the states of the government worker. Between 1947 and 1967, the number of public employees increased over 110 per cent [see table below]. (During the same period, private nonagricultural employment increased only 42 per cent.) Clearly, the day has passed when being a civil servant is a prestigious matter. At a time when unions and bargaining have become increasingly accepted elsewhere in the society, this expansion of public employment, with its consequent bureaucratization and depersonalization of relationships, has undoubtedly encouraged unionization in the public sector.

Public Employment Trends

	1947	1967
All Public Employment	5,474,000	11,616,000
Federal employment	1,892,000	2,719,000
State and local employment	3,582,000	8,897,000

A New Kind of Worker

The spread of unionism among government civil servants and teachers is a partial answer to the old question of whether substantial numbers of white-collar employees can be unionized. It is true that much of the growth of public unionism, principally the American Federation of State, County and Municipal Employees and the American Federation of Government Employees (which operates at the Federal level [see "The AFGE and the AFSCME," in Section II, below] has been among blue-collar employees. (Over two thirds of the AFL-CIO's State, County and Municipal Employees union, for example, are blue-collar workers.) But some important footholds have been gained among white-collar workers and (because teachers are the largest number unionized) among professionals.

Between 20 and 25 per cent of all local and state employees are teachers, and it is among them that the significant contest in unionization has been taking place. For the organization of teachers has had its impact not only in traditional union circles, but also among other associations of public service employees that formerly limited themselves to fraternal and professional questions. Prominent among these is the National Education Association (NEA). Under competition from the AFL-CIO American Federation of Teachers (AFT), the NEA has radically altered its views on bargaining in recent years. . . . [See "Why Teachers Are Striking," in Section III, below.]

Like the NEA, other independent state and local public employee associations whose activities until recently have largely been limited to welfare and fraternal programs, are now turning their attention to collective bargaining. These associations, strong among white-collar employees, include, at the state level alone, over 400,000 members who, in turn are loosely grouped into a national joint body. These associations have the additional advantage, in some states, of being favored by public managers.

As is clear from the many strikes reported, a great many different groups in the public sector are on the move. To the extent that one can judge, the new unrest seems to be greatest among those who have very clearly identifiable professions and/or strategic occupations. Teachers, for example, have clearly been in the forefront of public employee labor agitation in the past few years. Nurses have begun to make demands in the large cities. Social workers, a group with old traditions in public employee bargaining, are extending their organization significantly. Firemen and policemen have been revealing a new militancy. In their summer 1968 conventions the AFL-CIO's fireman's union and the independent American Nurses' Association both removed clauses prohibiting strikes from their respective constitutions. In contrast, such professional groups as engineers and architects (admittedly employed on a much smaller scale in the public sector than either teachers or nurses) are much less affected. These occupations continue to enjoy a generally more favorable labor market than the other professionals, and this would seem to be a clue to the difference.

Because it is likely that legislation encouraging collective bargaining in the near future will be enacted in more states, unionism at this level will clearly grow. The Department of Labor has projected that local and state employment will exceed 10 million by 1970, and unionism in this sector must almost inevitably grow in importance on the American labor scene.

The sharp increase in collective bargaining in the public service has served to offset the decline in traditional unionism. . . . Thus between 1956-1957 and 1966-1967 the AFL-CIO as a whole (including its rapidly growing government unions) made a modest recovery from its decline to the early 1960s and managed to increase its membership by 7 per cent. But during this same ten-year period public employee unions have doubled and tripled their membership. Even these figures, based as they are on biennial averages, understate the current membership for public employee unions. By the end of 1968 the American Federation of Government Employees (AFGE), which organized Federal workers, had jumped to 300,000. Some of AFGE's victories in bargaining-rights elections such as a 21,000 employee air base unit in September 1968 have been reminiscent of the CIO's organization of mass production industries of the late 1930s. The progress of the State, County and Municipal Workers (AFSCME) has been made in smaller units, but it had reached 400,000 late in 1968.

The rapid expansion of membership among the Federal unions, state, county, and municipal and teachers' unions has been accompanied by the sort of internal turmoil that usually goes with growth. Major conflicts for top union leadership positions have erupted in all three of these public employee unions during the past half dozen years. As membership rolls and treasuries expanded, moreover, and full-time elected and appointive posts opened up, struggles also occurred at the regional and local levels. With the prospect for continuing, substantial membership growth, we can expect relatively high instability and at least a fair amount of election conflict to continue among the officials of these unions.

We can also expect the leaders of the rapidly expanding public employee unions to move into larger roles in the top councils of the AFL-CIO itself. One reason why this has not been true up to now is the persistence of a long-standing conflict between the AFGE and some of the older, craft unions who want the AFGE to limit itself to white-collar, classified employees, and leave blue-collar unionizing in air bases, shipyards, ordinance depots, and the like to craft unions, notably the Metal Trades Council, which has long been active among these government employees. This the AFGE has refused to do. Early in 1967 it publicly opposed the official stand taken by the AFL-CIO (and the Metal Trades Council) before a congressional committee considering new legislation to reorganize those government wage boards which have the power to set wage rates for Federal blue-collar employees.

Still it cannot be long before some of the leaders of the leading public employee unions will be accorded seats on the AFL-CIO top executive council. Union size has always been one significant factor in the choice of the twenty-nine member council. The State, County, and Municipal Workers Union is already among the ten larger unions in terms of membership size. Its leader, the pugnacious Jerry Wurf [see "Strike Bans Warp Collective Bargaining," in Section IV, below] will probably receive a council seat. The American Federation of Government Employees may also be close to that level by the 1970 convention. Aside from size, the AFL-CIO will also stand to benefit from a more representative public image when teachers and other government employee representatives help to make up its executive council.

BLACK REVOLUTION AND
PUBLIC EMPLOYMENT [3]

Undoubtedly the greatest impact of the black revolution, or whatever name one chooses to give the refusal of Negro Americans to continue accepting the bottom rung on the American economic and social ladder, is in the area of public and nonprofit or charitable employment. During an era that followed craft and industrial manufacturing union organizing, we had a labor pattern that found unskilled, minority group men and women employed in the menial tasks of our society. Hospitals in the metropolitan eastern cities were perhaps the first institutions to face the dissatisfaction of the very low paid maintenance men and charwomen. Strikes in these institutions, both profit and nonprofit, established in many cities that this pool of unskilled and often casual workers could no longer be taken for granted.

Municipalities and other levels of government had also found minorities that last source of cheap manual labor. Street cleaners and garbage collectors have until recently been both unorganized and black. Or if not black, a counterpart minority group. Trace back the riots that erupted across our land from city to city last spring. They were touched off by the murder of Dr. Martin Luther King, who was slain in Memphis, where he had gone to help rally the cause of union recognition by the city of Memphis for the city's black garbage collectors.

Far from being model employers, as the Federal government tries to be, cities and other state subdivisions tend, if left alone, to pay the lowest wages they can to menial workers. Beset as they are by limited sources of funds, this situation is no surprise. But it is intolerable to men and women who no longer believe they are fated by nature to be the nation's permanent low-wage, slum-dwelling, propertyless class.

[3] From address, "A Government View of the State of Collective Bargaining," delivered by former Senator Wayne Morse (Democrat, Oregon) before the American Management Association Personnel Conference, New York City, February 4, 1969. The Association. New York. '69. Reprinted by permission.

The Congress came to grips with its share of this problem in 1966 by extending minimum wage standards to several types of local governmental employees.

For this group of Americans, who their employer is, is of much less importance than the fact that their wage scales are below white standards. Their *need* to bargain collectively is not disputable. But the means at hand, and the adverse attitude of a public that considers municipal services an inviolable right, are big obstacles. This group of workers is not likely, however, to accept less by way of bargaining than industrial workers.

In a somewhat different category are the more professional public employees—policemen and teachers. Their rising militancy is not unlike that of minority employees. They, too, feel left out of the general upward surge of affluence. Many of them believe that militancy has paid off for others, and it is time for them to begin making and enforcing their own demands.

Few states have more stringent laws against strikes by public employees than New York. Few states have been more beset by strikes by public employees, despite the law. In fact, the stiff jail penalties have seemed so out of line with the offense that the law has become inoperative in many of these situations. It has been evaded, too, by such roundabout strike devices as large numbers of policemen "calling in sick."

Lacking the general protection of the National Labor Relations Act, public employees have been looking for their own means of achieving collective bargaining status. This search is bound to continue. Certainly the states and cities that do not have them will have to devise procedures and systems for negotiating with organizations of public employees. Expanded use of voluntary arbitration is, in my opinion, one of the more promising alternatives in the labor-management relations between employees and a public entity.

Labor relations in the public sector, too, is a changing situation that calls for trial and error, some experimentation, and time to acquire experience. I doubt that it calls for national legislation as yet.

II. UNIONS IN PUBLIC EMPLOYMENT

EDITOR'S INTRODUCTION

In the fall of 1969 a news report told of efforts by Foreign Service officers of the Department of State to form an organization to bargain collectively with their superiors in the Department. At the same time, field examiners in the National Labor Relations Board (of all places) were having their difficulties seeking representation with their "employer."

Bizarre as these examples may have seemed only a few years ago, they are symbolic of the role of collective bargaining by unions of government employees. This section deals with these unions, beginning with the two largest organizations, as described in the first article by Harry A. Donoian. Policemen's and firefighters' unions, obviously of a special nature, are described by J. Joseph Loewenberg.

The articles by Robert Lewis, Darryl Mleynek, and Keith M. Cottam take up the matter of unions among library employees, the first providing step-by-step details of the negotiations of an initial contract, quite typical of such activity in public sector union-management relations.

The Tennessee Valley Authority, a "yardstick" in public power generation, has also provided a long-standing example of labor-management relations, described by Aubrey J. Wagner, TVA board chairman. Finally, Archie Kleingartner's selection on nurses indirectly makes a different point: Nurses, like many other types of workers (sanitation workers and bus drivers, for example), are frequently public employees, but in other contexts employees of private companies or institutions—nonprofit or profit-oriented. Such workers (and their unions) ask the basic question: Should the nurse, garbage man, or bus driver who works for a municipality be treated

differently from the same type of worker employed by a non-
government employer?

THE AFGE AND THE AFSCME [1]

To get some idea as to what the future holds for public
employee unionism it might be well to examine the two largest unions in the field, the American Federation of State,
County and Municipal Employees (AFSCME) and the
American Federation of Government Employees (AFGE),
both affiliated with the AFL-CIO. Not only are these two
unions the largest but the AFSCME and the AFGE have the
greatest possibility for future growth because of the jurisdiction that has been allotted them by the AFL-CIO and because of their past growth records.

The jurisdiction provided for in the AFSCME constitution consists of employees "of any state, territory, township,
or other public authority, except elected officials" and employees "of any quasi-public agency or any nonprofit or tax
exempt agency of a public, charitable, educational, or civic
nature." Thus, the AFSCME feels itself free to organize just
about anyone in the nonindustry, noncommercial labor
force, excluding the Federal Government. The AFGE claims
jurisdiction over all civilian employees of the United States
Government and the District of Columbia "excepting those
over whom jurisdiction has been granted to other national
or international unions by the American Federation of
Labor and the Congress of Industrial Organizations.

A concomitant of wide jurisdictions for both the
AFSCME and AFGE has been jurisdictional disputes with
other AFL-CIO unions. There have been a number of different ones but the most significant have involved the Building Service Employees' International Union against the
AFSCME, and the AFL-CIO's Metal Trades Department and

[1] From "The AFGE and the AFSCME: Labor's Hope for the Future?" by
Harry A. Donoian, labor economist, Bureau of Labor Statistics, United States
Department of Labor. *Labor Law Journal.* 18:727-38. D. '67. Reprinted by
permission.

the International Association of Machinists against the AFGE.

These disputes have arisen, in large part, because of the kind of organizing technique that both unions use. The AFSCME and the AFGE can both be classified as industrial unions with both belonging to the AFL-CIO's Industrial Union Department. Organizing does not have a place, however, on strictly industrial lines. Rather, a free form of organization has developed where both unions issue charters to virtually any group not affiliated which shows a willingness to belong to the organization. In other words, craft and industrial locals are formed on the basis of the wishes of those applying for charters. Both unions, however, are industrial in the sense that all workers within the general jurisdiction outlined above are accepted for membership, not just those in a particular craft. Both unions have large groups of white- and blue-collar employees as members. . . .

Both unions were chartered during the 1930s. . . . The geneses of the two unions were significantly different, however. One arose because of a controversy within the AFL, the other because of a movement of workers in a particular area.

Jurisdiction over Federal employees not covered by any craft unions was given to the National Federation of Federal Employees (NFFE) in 1917 by the American Federation of Labor. The NFFE withdrew from the AFL in 1931 because of a dispute with the AFL's Metal Trades Department at the AFL convention that year over personnel classification legislation. To cover this jurisdiction, the AFGE was chartered by the AFL on August 18, 1932, with about two thousand former members of the original NFFE in thirty-nine lodges. For many years the NFFE was by far the larger of the two unions. . . . In more recent years, membership in the . . . [AFGE] has far outstripped that in the . . . [NFFE]. . . . In fact, the NFFE was in a period of severe decline until the signing of Executive Order 10988 by President Kennedy in 1962. . . . [See "Executive Order 10988," in Section V, below.] The AFGE, with backing from the AFL-CIO's Industrial

Union Department, has probably enjoyed the greatest benefits from the Executive Order, however.

The AFSCME was chartered by the AFL on October 16, 1936, but the seed that produced this organization had been planted in Wisconsin some four years before. On May 16, 1932, the AFL issued a charter to Federal Labor Union 18213 which adopted the name "Wisconsin State Employees Association." This organization began the push for the establishment of a national union representing state and local employees and was led by Arnold S. Zander, who was to become for many years the president of the AFSCME. Efforts to establish a national union in the AFL to represent state and local government ran into difficulties because the AFL had granted this jurisdiction to the AFGE in 1934.

In December 1935, the AFGE convention voted to establish the AFSCME as an autonomous union within the AFGE with their own constitution and officers. Over the course of the following year, the AFGE recognized the differences between the two organizations and . . . voted . . . to divest the organization of the state and local jurisdiction. . . . The AFSCME became an independent national union soon after, by virtue of AFL Executive Council action.

Strategy and Tactics

The one area of operations of the AFSCME and the AFGE where there is probably the greatest difference is in the matter of strategy and tactics. It is generally believed that public employee unions have two basic weapons at their disposal. These are passage of legislative acts improving the circumstances of employment and direct collective bargaining. Neither union depends exclusively on one of these tools but it appears that the AFSCME relies more heavily on collective bargaining as it is used in private industry while the AFGE is more partial to legislative activity. The difference in tactics and strategy is attributable, at least in part, to the different institutional arrangements with which these organizations must contend.

Collective bargaining is viewed by the AFSCME as the most appropriate means of securing its goals. The AFSCME constitution specifically states that one of its objectives is "to promote the welfare of the membership and to provide a voice in the determination of the terms and conditions of employment." To secure that end the union is "committed to the process of collective bargaining as the most desirable, democratic, and effective method to achieve this."

An even more militant position on collective bargaining was taken by the AFSCME International Executive Board. In a policy statement adopted July 26, 1966, the Board stated in part that:

We believe that good labor-management relations in government, as in the private sector of the economy, must be concerned with fundamental problems and fundamental relations. The certification and collective bargaining processes used in private industry have worked well, where tried, in the public area. They can be improved and expanded in the public employment by the continued application of sound principles. Public officials must recognize that they must deal with the problems of their employees, not sweep them under the rug and hope they will stay out of sight. If public officials and public employee unions approach the problem responsibly, sound solutions will be found. Collective bargaining does work in the public interest. . . .

This analogy with private sector collective bargaining is taken one step further by the AFSCME. The union insists upon the right of government employees, with the exception of police officers, to strike. The right to strike is essential because the union believes that the collective bargaining process is dependent upon a power relationship and "where one party at the bargaining table possesses all the power and authority, bargaining becomes no more than formalized petitioning." The AFSCME believes that forestalling the right to strike seriously cripples the free collective bargaining process. The Board states that it is policy of the International to remove the legal barriers to strike action wherever they exist. . . .

While the AFSCME sees the value of mediation and third-person fact finding, it totally rejects the concept of arbitrating bargaining disputes. It feels that "the will to reach an agreement must be present at the table." Also, it does not wish to abandon "to strangers the final voice in determining the wages and working conditions of our membership."

Where the AFSCME constitution put an emphasis on collective bargaining, the AFGE constitution emphasizes legislative action. Article II, Objects and Methods, Section 2 states that "the Federation shall strive to promote efficiency in the governmental service, and shall advance plans of improvement to be secured by legislative enactment through cooperation with governmental officials and other lawful means." There is no mention of collective bargaining in the AFGE constitution although Section 3 of Article II does mention strikes. This section states that "the American Federation of Government Employees is opposed to and will not engage in strikes against Government authority." ...

Virtually all Federal employees . . . have their pay determined by congressional action. Similarly, Congress has jurisdiction over basic employee benefits such as annual and sick leave, compensation for injury, insurance, and employer contributions to health and welfare plans. Until Congress relinquishes authority over these areas, the only way that unions which represent Federal Government employees can secure increased pay and improved benefits is to use legislative tactics. The possibility of Congress relinquishing this authority in the near future is quite remote. . . .

Where the AFSCME can advocate and use power in their relationships with employers because of relatively greater closeness between state and local administrative units and their respective legislative bodies, the AFGE cannot. There is a wide gap between the local administrative agency where collective bargaining pressure could be brought to bear and the Congress of the United States, and the pressure which could be brought to bear at the local level is not transferable to the national level. . . .

The situation which the AFGE faces is not unique to it. All Federal "employee organizations" are in the same position. What the union has done is to adopt the same strategy and tactics which have proven so successful for the postal unions. . . .

The AFSCME is active on many fronts besides the collective bargaining arena. It lobbies on the state and local level to get legislation passed which would be favorable to its members. This latter function is an important role of the union's state councils. The current thrust of the AFSCME's legislative efforts relates to improving collective bargaining conditions and safeguarding the position of the union. In the former area, the AFSCME seeks to have laws passed authorizing collective bargaining between unions and public employers, while in the latter the union presses for passage of measures permitting such things as checkoff of union dues. . . .

Future Prospects

It is expected that the future will see both unions using collective bargaining so far as possible under the relevant statutes, although the AFGE will still be putting a large share of their national office efforts in the legislative area. Indeed, the AFSCME may, in all probability, exceed some of the legal limitations put on public employee union activity, particularly in the matter of strikes. The possibility of the AFGE doing the same in the near future is nonexistent.

Both the AFSCME and the AFGE should continue to grow. The rate at which both organizations become larger will probably be in direct proportion to the extent that both unions capture the mood of employees in their jurisdictions. During the past several years, they have apparently done this well. The AFSCME and the AFGE probably may do as well in the future, if they keep abreast of rising employee expectations which will probably continue to rise. . . .

Public employee unionism is here to stay. The efforts of such organizations as the International Association of Ma-

chinists, Building Service Employees International Union,
Postal Unions, American Federation of Teachers, AFL-CIO's
Metal Trades Department, and International Association of
Firefighters, besides those of the AFSCME and the AFGE
have permanently established a place for unions in the civil
service structure. Both the AFSCME and the AFGE should
be among the leading public service employee unions.
Whether they will be *the* leaders will depend on their re-
sourcefulness and their adaptability.

POLICEMEN AND FIREFIGHTERS [2]

Policemen and firefighters have the reputation for impressive group cohesion. In the early history of many departments, this cohesiveness led to the formation of employee social and benefit organizations. Some continue to function according to their original purpose and structure. Others have
changed over the years.

Firefighters formed the International Association of Fire
Fighters (IAFF) as an affiliate of the American Federation of
Labor in 1918. It is by far the largest and most influential
organization of firefighters, with about half of all paid firefighters as members. The jurisdiction of the organization includes professional firefighters of all ranks except those
working in shipyard fire departments; it also excludes non-
uniformed employees of fire departments. As a union, the
IAFF has recently conducted seminars to promote collective bargaining concepts to local union representatives. Since
1930, however, its constitution has contained a no-strike
clause.

At the national level, the activities of the union are circumscribed. The International staff consists of sixteen people
in Washington. Per capita dues (65 cents a month) are the
lowest of any union in the United States. Fifteen vice presidents, each in charge of a geographic area, are fire department

[2] From "Labor Relations for Policemen and Firefighters," by J. Joseph
Loewenberg, assistant professor, Department of Management, Temple University. *Monthly Labor Review*. 91:36-40. My. '68.

employees and thus can devote only part time to organizing, representing the union in state legislatures, and performing other duties of an executive board member. This leaves locals with considerable autonomy in policy and operating decisions.

For policemen, the development and current status of employee organizations is quite different. Greater initial wariness of policemen by the labor movement, and reactions to police employee organizations following the 1919 Boston police strike, long derailed efforts for any widespread organization. Nevertheless, policemen did continue to organize. They were more likely to fragment on a rank basis than firemen, with separate organizations for patrolmen, detectives, and various officer groups.

FOP, the Fraternal Order of Police, was founded in 1915 but did not significantly add to its membership until the 1930s. Today it is the largest national police employee organization. Policemen of all ranks are eligible for membership in FOP. Associate memberships are available to the general public. The organization's original purposes were directed toward securing civil service protection and bolstering pension systems through lobbying. In time, local FOP lodges expanded their interests to all police monetary items and working conditions and also emphasized recreational facilities and activities. The only full-time member of the national staff is the president. Because it is not affiliated with the AFL-CIO, the FOP does not consider itself a labor union. It ensures autonomy for local lodges and maintains a substantially lower dues structure than AFL-CIO unions.

The National Conference of Police Associations was established to act as a coordinating agency for autonomous local police organizations. Its annual survey of police wages and working conditions parallels the effort of the Fraternal Order of Police.

Meanwhile, national labor unions have not left organization of policemen completely untended. The American Federation of State, County and Municipal Employees has attempted to organize policemen with mixed success. Today the union's principal strength is in Connecticut and Illinois. Policemen usually belong to separate locals, but they are also found in locals with other employees.

Both the service employees and the teamsters have active locals of uniformed policemen. It is the rule of some police locals that the charter will be revoked if policemen "strike or refuse in concert to perform their duties."

The confusion in police employee organizations extends beyond their numbers. Local organizations sometimes change affiliations and dual memberships in organizations are not uncommon for policemen.

As public employees, policemen and firefighters are exempt from the Federal statutes and machinery that protect the organizing rights of most workers in the private sector of the economy.

Legal Framework

State legislation affecting organizing and bargaining rights of public employees has increased rapidly in recent years. The pressures of policemen and firefighter employee organizations have not been different from other public employee organizations. Organizing and bargaining among public employees continues to be limited.

One of the major changes introduced by most recent statutes is to give public employee organizations the right to bargain on behalf of their represented employees with the duly constituted authorities. Such bargaining had not been unknown before, but it was generally resisted. There is still a relatively small amount of enabling legislation, and usually where there are such laws, policemen and firemen are excluded or have special restrictions placed on them. Department officials feared that bargaining was a contradiction of the role of protective service employees. If the organization had any role in employee matters, it was likely to be restricted to presenting views on salary before municipal authorities and to lobbying at local and state levels.

The variety of definitions given to collective bargaining makes it hazardous to calculate the extent of bargaining. A recent survey indicates that of 603 cities with IAFF locals in their fire departments, 314 report bargaining. There is no significant difference by size of city in the proportion of cities with locals bargaining; smaller cities were much less likely to have IAFF locals, however. As more states provide protective service employees with bargaining rights and experience cumulates, the extent of collective bargaining is likely to increase rapidly. Individual cities have chosen to bargain without state legislation, and pressure from employee organizations to extend collective bargaining by this route may also grow. . . .

At the very heart of the bargaining process is the subject matter for bargaining. Some negotiations are concerned only with economic matters; others go much further in regulating working conditions.

As long as the governing authorities provide sufficient resources, the results of economic bargaining are perhaps of less concern to department officials than are other parts of the negotiations. In fact, department officials may support wage increases as a means of improving morale and aiding recruiting efforts. Such items as overtime pay, callback pay, and pay for temporary service out of rank may challenge department management and department budgets, however, and are not unrelated to the time-off provisions that have been negotiated.

Other negotiated items may affect department operations more directly and are therefore of greater concern to department officials. Bidding systems for promotions, role of seniority, and substitution of work assignments have been negotiated in some instances, though often with restrictions. Many police and fire department officials object to the inclusion of such items in negotiations.

The role and rights of the employee organization are also usually considered negotiable subjects, particularly the role of the organization in grievances. All forms of union security have been negotiated. For example, union-shop agreements are not uncommon in Connecticut and Rhode Island police departments; an agency shop [in which employees not belonging to the union must pay a "service fee" to the union] exists in the Rochester (New York) police and fire departments; and a maintenance-of-membership provision has been negotiated in the Detroit police department.

As significant as negotiated subjects are topics that management has held to be nonnegotiable. According to management, the subjects concern department efficiency and management responsibility and therefore are wholly within its discretion. Included in this category are the size of the work force, the number of men in a squad, manning of work stations including patrol cars, selection of assignment, maintenance of residential requirement for employment, and moonlighting. (Selection of work assignment has been included, if rarely, in the negotiable list.)

Employee organizations do not always agree that a subject is nonnegotiable and they sometimes seek their demands through other channels. When moonlighting was declared nonnegotiable in New York City, the patrolmen successfully lobbied for state legislative authority.

Considering the similarity of problems and benefits of policemen and firefighters, it might appear logical for organizations representing the two groups to work closely together during negotiations. This rarely happens. The rivalry between the groups sometimes hampers effective collective bargaining. In one city, the policemen's organization purposefully protracted negotiations to obtain a long-term agreement which appeared to offer higher wages than had been given to firefighters.

There have been exceptions to the lack of joint bargaining. A notable example occurred in New York City in 1966 when the Uniformed Firemen's Association and Patrolmen's Benevolent Association presented their demands to the city jointly and insisted on joint negotiations until agreement was reached. The two organizations remained together, even though the negotiations went to fact finding and eventually, when the firefighters threatened to strike, to the mayor. Most bargaining alliances are temporary, and even then they are tenuous.

If policemen and firefighters do not bargain jointly, they pay close attention to the results of the others' bargaining. It is common practice to insert a "savings" clause requiring the political authority to grant wages and economic benefits negotiated with other units of the protective service departments during the same fiscal year.

Although the leading employee organizations have disavowed the use of the strike as a tactical weapon, in ... [recent] years there have been strikes lasting from 5 hours to 5 days in the fire departments of Atlanta; Kansas City; Danville, Illinois; and Saginaw, Michigan; in the police departments of Joliet, Illinois; Detroit; and Pontiac, Michigan; and in fire and police departments simultaneously in Youngstown, Ohio. The technical form of the work stoppage was mass resignation, calling in sick, continuing professional meetings, or simply a walkout. The employee organizations involved were independent associations and affiliates of IAFF and FOP. The issue in all cases except one was economic, and the exception concerned discipline administered for pressure tactics used to influence wage bargaining. There have also been several threatened strikes, including one by New York City firefighters which was supported by the Central Labor Council.

In several situations, employers have responded strongly to pressure tactics. The strike of an independent employee organization led by two captains against the Atlanta Fire Department in 1966 resulted in suspension and dismissal of over half of the force; some of those who were fired were later rehired as new employees, together with a large number of new recruits. Suspensions were also meted out in the Detroit Police Department to those who participated in a slowdown of writing tickets and who abused sick-leave privileges. Saginaw authorities docked the pay of firefighters who used sick leave to stage a walkout. In most cases, however, including the five-day strike in Youngstown, there appears to have been no retaliatory measures against those who used pressure tactics. . . .

The emergence of collective bargaining for policemen and firefighters has not ended their efforts to lobby for improved benefits and working conditions. Although lobbying activity varies, there is little question that it is widespread and that it affects collective bargaining.

Employee organizations will bear much of the burden for the future course of collective bargaining. Their present attitude toward collective bargaining is often ambivalent, as exemplified by frequent recourse to lobbying with local or state legislators. While such tactics yield the desired objective, they weaken the "good faith" bargaining relationship. Old habits are hard to break, particularly if they prove successful. Employee organizations must decide whether they want bargaining to work or to be reduced to another political football.

The plans of public safety department administrators affect employees and hence collective bargaining. Similarly, the content and conduct of collective bargaining can affect department operations. Administrators who stand by silently while bargaining alters their operational efficiency cannot shrug off the blame on the system. Administrators must also learn that they can promote efficiency through collective bargaining. But this requires involvement, and with involvement comes, it is hoped, knowledge and understanding.

NEGOTIATING A LIBRARY UNION CONTRACT [3]

Almost lost in the excitement surrounding the growth of public employee unionization has been the vigorous union

[3] From "A New Dimension in Library Administration—Negotiating a Union Contract," by Robert Lewis, partner, Jackson, Lewis, Schnitzler & Krupman, the firm retained by the Brooklyn Public Library to negotiate the contract discussed in this article. *ALA Bulletin*. 63:455-64. Ap. '69. Reprinted by permission.

organizing efforts directed at the quasi-public employee. The rapid growth of unionization among teachers, nurses, and social workers has all but hidden the union organizing attempts in the quasi-public employment field.

The term *quasi-public* as used here defines those employees working for public service employers, or whose employment is associated with a public endeavor. This class is well illustrated by the employees of the cultural institutions of New York City. In New York, the zoological societies, botanical gardens, museums, and libraries are each private corporate institutions supported in part and in varying amounts by public funds and operated to provide a cultural benefit available to all residents of the city.

Most notable of all the organizing efforts has been the vigorous drive to organize employees in the public library systems, in particular, the professional librarian classifications. . . .

Union organizing at the [Brooklyn Public] Library started early in 1966 with a campaign by District Council 37 of the American Federation of State, County and Municipal Employees, AFL-CIO, commonly referred to as AFSCME. This campaign was conducted in an atmosphere conducive to the union's cause. Public employees throughout New York City had gained recognition by the city government; and the New York City public school system, having recently granted recognition to the teachers' union, had just acceded to that union's demands for substantial improvements in benefits. At the very same time, civil service employees throughout New York State were undergoing intensive organizing by the AFSCME, the Civil Service Employees' Association, and several other unions active in the public employee field. The state government was publicly drafting legislation to accommodate this ground swell of organization among employees engaged in the public service. It was therefore not surprising when, in June 1966, the Board of Trustees of the library was presented with a demand for recognition by District Council 37, AFSCME.

The Board of Trustees met with representatives of the union and was presented with the union's claim that it represented a majority of the library's employees in all professional librarian, clerical, maintenance, and custodial titles.

In New York City, a cultural institution such as a library could elect to come under the New York City collective bargaining statutes which provides a mechanism for determining the collective bargaining representative of the institution's employees. In the alternative, the library was free to follow any other election mechanism, including those practiced by private industry. Since the library was not covered by either Federal, state, or city labor relations laws, it possessed a greater freedom of choice of method than other public libraries or private enterprise employers.

The library chose to utilize the services of the New York City Department of Labor. A secret ballot election was held to determine whether a majority of its employees wished to be represented by the union requesting recognition.

An Election Is Held

In the fall of 1966, an election was conducted among two separate units or groupings of employees. The first unit was composed of all professional librarians throughout the system with the exception of major administrative officers of the library. The second unit was composed of all residual classifications, comprised mainly of the clerical and maintenance staffs. . . .

The election results demonstrated that the union was successful in selling its program. While it failed to produce the resounding tally the union hoped for, it succeeded in achieving the required majority in each of the two election units.

Following quickly on the heels of the election was the union's demand to institute the device to make dues collections easy by a dues checkoff among the employees. The union also asked for the establishment of a formalized grievance procedure. . . .

The library had selected a well-balanced committee of three top administrators as its representatives. Labor relations counsel was then chosen to attend with them at the bargaining table. The three administrators selected were the Deputy Director, the Executive Assistant to the Director, and the Personnel Director. The committee, of course, reported to the Director, who reviewed the union's proposals, the administration's counterproposals and contributed his views to both the committee and its counsel prior to each subsequent meeting with the union. . . .

The union was represented by one of its staff spokesmen who articulated the union's views. Five library employees comprised the union's bargaining committee. . . .

First Demands of the Union

A set of preliminary demands was submitted to the administration in January of 1967. The union's initial requests centered upon substituting itself in place of the long established Brooklyn Public Library Staff Association. This Association had, for many years, been a voluntary membership organization open to all library employees. It had as its primary function the organization of library social events and the fostering of professional activities as well as participation on the library's promotion board. Some of the officers of the Association became officers of the union. The union thus would wish to see itself as the successor to the Staff Association, with all the rights, benefits, and privileges which the library had accorded to the Association. During the course of negotiations it was particularly difficult to convince the union representatives that the union was not in fact a successor to the Association, but was actually a new entity which had a separate and distinct legal relationship with the library and its employees.

This successorship problem became readily apparent in a preliminary set of demands which the union submitted. These included, in addition to the request for dues checkoff and a grievance procedure, the following benefits which the

Association had enjoyed: (1) Use of library bulletin boards to publicize union activity; (2) Use of internal interbranch mail system to distribute union material; (3) Distribution by the library, to all new employees, of union literature and an application for membership; and (4) The use of working time and library facilities to conduct union business.

The library resisted these requests because of the obvious encroachment that the granting of these requests would have on service to the public. Of equal importance was the fact that the granting of these privileges would in effect make the library administration an agent of the union in conducting union affairs, communication with members, and recruiting new members. . . .

The Hard Issues of Collective Bargaining

By April of 1967, the parties had resolved the procedural aspects of negotiations and had negotiated an interim understanding on dues checkoff and a grievance procedure. The union then submitted a list of thirty-two proposals. Many of these items were the pro forma demands usually made for a first contract, such as a recognition clause and a clause providing for nondiscrimination by the library because of an employee's union membership. The other items fell basically into two categories: employee benefits and union rights. . . .

Economic Improvements. The library was in a unique position in terms of the economic requests made of it by the union. Since the City of New York is the source of funds to pay for such items, the library could not engage in meaningful negotiations in regard to economic items, because any agreement would of necessity require subsequent budgetary approval by the City, a matter which was far from automatic. Recognizing that the union would be obligated to negotiate directly with the City on these matters, the parties agreed that the scope of collective bargaining on employee benefits would be limited to noneconomic matters. At such time as the union negotiated an agreement with the City to provide and allocate funds for economic items such as night shift differentials, overtime premiums, uniform and work clothes allowances, and most significantly, increases in salary, the library would agree to reopen negotiations with the union in regard only to the implementation of such benefits. With this important matter out of the way, the parties proceeded to negotiate over the noneconomic aspects of employment conditions.

Noneconomic Benefits: Past Practice Clause. The union initially requested a "past practices" clause whereby the library would agree to keep in effect all favorable practices and benefits which it had extended in the past to its employees.

The library was counseled not to grant such a clause. To do so would be to agree to a blanket continuation of any and all practices, known and unknown. In effect, the union was asking the library to buy a "pig-in-the-poke," a commodity the library did not seek to purchase. To the extent that the union was capable of enumerating and defining those practices which it sought to continue, the library's position was that they would be negotiable. Therefore, this request was rejected and not included in the contract.

The library did agree, however, to continue the existing administrative Rules Affecting Personnel which, in the future, the library would change only after consultation with the union. It was evident that as to these existing practices, both the union and the library were capable of making direct and specific reference, thereby avoiding the possibility of misunderstandings so common when the parties to a negotiation agree to a clause to continue past practices.

Miscellaneous Noneconomic Benefits. In evidence at the negotiations were the minor points which each of the union negotiators sought to win for their own job classifications which they represented. The maintenance and custodial employees made a strong point of requesting special payment for employees called in to shovel snow away from branch entrances or do other emergency repair or maintenance work.

The issue of snow removal consumed a considerable amount of negotiating time and ultimately resulted in a codification of existing rules which permitted crediting the employee with a minimum number of hours for each call-in, for which he was given compensating time off. The magnitude of this union effort was utterly misplaced in view of the fact that during the past year only one employee had suffered any inconvenience because of snow removal.

The Temperature Humidity Index. We will not get into a discourse on the theoretical physical properties of a hygrometer. Suffice it to say that the reading on this instrument gives a factor known as the THI or temperature humidity index.

Several negotiating sessions were spent in seemingly endless discussions on the conditions under which library branches would be closed because of adverse weather conditions [and a detailed agreement was worked out based on THI readings]. . . .

Time and Leave Regulations. Matters of time and leave provisions were relatively easy to resolve. Maternity leave was extended for an additional six months and bereavement leave was extended to cover the death of additional members of an employee's immediate family. The library agreed to grant nonpaid leave time to a limited number of union members to attend union meetings and conventions.

As has been pointed out, many of the benefits which the union proposed were already in existence at the library. For example, the union asked for a specified number of annual paid holidays which in fact coincided with the library's existing holiday policy. The union also requested that in the event of illness, employees be permitted to liquidate all their accrued sick leave before utilizing accrued vacation leave. This, too, was already an existing benefit. . . .

Seniority Provisions. A disquieting note in the union's approach to negotiations was the constant reliance upon seniority as a controlling factor for matters of professional development as well as the distribution of benefits. The union sought to make all interbranch transfers and the scheduling of vacations based solely on seniority rather than taking into consideration that vacation schedules would require the maintenance of adequate staff to serve the public. This cannot always be on the basis of granting the requests of the employee who has the longest service. Transfers of librarians from one branch to another were frequently made so that the librarian could broaden his professional experience. The union, however, sought to limit the administration's discretion in this matter by gearing interbranch transfers directly to a seniority system. The library succeeded in having the union drop the demand that seniority must prevail.

Union Participation on Library's Promotion Board. The issue of participation on the library's promotion board was pressed as a matter of major concern for the union and was one of the last items resolved by the parties. The library properly viewed the union's participation in selecting employees for promotion as an incursion of the library's managerial prerogatives. The union, on the other hand, sought to justify their demands by claiming a successorship to the staff association, which had formerly designated two members to the seven-man promotion board. The matter was ultimately resolved by excluding the issue of promotions entirely from the scope of collective bargaining covered by the contract; but at the same time the library agreed to allow the union to participate to a limited extent in the selection of some of the staff representatives on the promotion board. . . .

Arbitration of Grievances. The incorporation of . . . [an] interim grievance procedure into the collective bargaining agreement required resolution of the union's demand for arbitration. The library took the position that there could be no arbitration clause without a meaningful no-strike commitment by the union [which was agreed upon]. The need for such a commitment was demonstrated throughout the negotiations by the union's overt and implied threats to strike, picket, or demonstrate. The union provided further credence to this possibility by the public pronouncements of the Executive Director of District Council 37, AFSCME, who publicly stated that he would even defy the no-strike ban in the recently enacted [New York State] Taylor Law.

The possibility of strikes, slowdowns, and other forms of union pressure during the term of a contract is not peculiar to public employment alone. It is a commonplace in industrial relations generally. Notwithstanding grievance and arbitration provisions in a collective bargaining agreement, unions have struck rather than follow the prescribed peaceful procedure. With this in mind, the library . . . [obtained] meaningful and enforceable penalty provisions in its contract should the union strike. . . .

The penalties against both the employees and . . . the union are fully enforceable in court and outside the scope of arbitration. Employee penalties are in the area of disciplinary action which includes discharge. Union penalties are in the form of monetary damages. In both instances, the penalties are excluded from the jurisdiction of an arbitrator where the propriety of the library's actions would be subject to question and "equitable" defenses.

Thus, after seven months of negotiations, the first union contract covering an entire library system in New York City was agreed upon. Needless to say, nationwide organizing efforts among librarians are continuing at an accelerated pace. Thus, union organizing and labor relations is now a matter of major concern for library administrators throughout the country. Truly, library administration throughout the country has taken on a new dimension.

UNION ROLE IN LIBRARY PROGRESS [4]

The formation of a union has traditionally threatened management rather seriously. . . . Management has often suddenly championed an immediate pay raise or a shorter work week in order to undercut a union's arguments, or they have attempted to dictate which classes of employees could join the union and which could not, or any one of many other harassing tactics. Normally, these measures have only served to delay the formation of the union and to add to existing hostilities, making future progress much more difficult.

This traditional pattern is still typical in the contemporary labor movement, although not necessarily between unions and library administrators. The union movement within libraries is far too new to talk much about patterns. It is worth noting, however, that in some of the libraries on the East Coast, library administrators did jump into the traditional management role. The result was many long, frustrating years for everybody within these systems. In the end, the unions largely won, although management did gain a few additional years without unions. However, they paid heavily for this time because they had helped to create deep cleavages within their libraries by encouraging the establishment of opposing sides with solidified positions. Predictably, many years yet of distrust and defensiveness will pass before the natural ties of a common profession win out and bring about a sense of unity of purpose.

In other cases of the formation of library unions—especially on the West Coast, the administrators have welcomed the union, according it all of the hospitality and all of the amenities that a library association would be given. The result of this attitude is obvious: a reservoir of good will has been built up which will carry the union and administrators

[4] From "Unions—What's in It for Administrators?" by Darryl Mleynek, former president of the Librarians' Guild, Local 1634, and former reference librarian, Social Science Department, Los Angeles Public Library. *Wilson Library Bulletin.* 43:752-5. Ap. '69. Reprinted by permission.

through the many legitimate problems that will arise in the coming years.

What's an Administrator to Do?

There are, then, two basic postures that a library administrator can take if he sees a union of his professional staff looming up: (1) He can try to block the formation of the union through the use of a series of frustrating tactics; or (2) he can cooperate with the union.

The futility of the first reaction is easily illustrated by two nearly self-evident facts: the first of these is that, much like politicians, management seems to have a natural tendency to blame all disturbances on outside agitators. But, as we who have been involved in these disturbances know, it just isn't the case. No union is going to come in and organize a library's staff. Quite the contrary, if there is a union in a library's future, it will be the library's staff who did the organizational work and who provided the motivation for the union's development. The union's part, once the staff has contacted them, will only be to provide advice, some money for literature and mailings, and strong backing should any difficulties develop. Secondly, before a library staff invests as heavily in money, time, and emotional energy as the organization of a union requires, it almost undoubtedly will have some very real complaints. . . .

If in the course of events an administrator is suddenly confronted with a union and, further, if he is able to fight off any natural reactions of panic and, further yet, if he adopts a stance of cooperation, then there are several areas in which the union can help him out.

Many administrators have worked for higher wages for their staff, as well as for a shorter work week, longer vacations, better working conditions, sabbatical leaves, and a program of continuing education. These are, after all, some of the immediate and long-range goals of most library administrators. And, of course, they are also the goals of library unions.

As the profession exists now though, each administrator fights for these goals largely on his own, expressing through letters and maybe even personal appearances the needs of the staff to his board and perhaps to a city council or a county board of supervisors. The task of presenting these matters to politicians who are going to make political decisions is obviously quite difficult, especially when the chief librarian lacks any independent political power. Surely the low salaries of librarians in comparison to other professional groups clearly illustrates these difficulties. . . .

Since administrators are plagued by a high staff turnover rate, low morale, and an inability to fill vacancies, all of which are due in part to poor wages, it would seem to be of some advantage to them to have an independent group also fighting for wage increases. And wouldn't it be especially helpful if that group could do the kind of lobbying that chief librarians aren't free to do? That could develop its own public relations campaign? That could work within a set of well-established laws set up for this purpose?

Of course, to administrators it may not appear that simple. They may, for instance, fear that a union would push for higher wages at the expense of the book budget or some other important item. However, a union of librarians is also a professional group. They will not have sold out their responsibility to the library and the community merely because they banded together in a union. In fact, their responsibility will almost undoubtedly increase. As a result of union activities, they will become both more involved in and more knowledgeable about the library's problems. Involvement begets professionalism; and professionalism is almost by definition responsibility. For this very reason, there is a new movement among library union members to limit their membership to professional librarians. This, for instance, has been done by the Librarians' Guild, Local 1634, American Federation of State, County and Municipal Employees, AFL-CIO, with chapters at the Los Angeles Public Library, San Francisco Public Library, and Santa Monica Public Library.

Such unions might be called professional unions—that is, unions of professionals—with interests running along professional lines and not being solely restricted to salaries and working conditions. They are interested in the broad formulation of policy and goals; in improving communications within the library in order that all librarians can effectively represent the library to the public and in order that problems of the administration and of the staff are known to each other; in extending service to the disadvantaged and all other groups not presently being served; and in being in a position to defend the library effectively against those who do not approve of or understand what librarians are doing.

In each of these broad areas, library unions are working as strong professional organizations. The strength and independence that is necessary to be effective in these areas have been borrowed from the union movement. However, *what* library unions work for comes straight from the library world. . . . Do not be misled into believing that a union hierarchy determines policy for a local of librarians. They do not. A union local composed entirely of librarians sets its own policy. The union's role is only to help them achieve the goals that they themselves establish. . . .

Librarians [should not] feel that all unions are the agents of reactionary forces as Karl Nyren suggested in an editorial in the November 1, 1968, issue of *Library Journal*. It is true that Governor Wallace found some support among blue-collar union members and it is also true that some unions no longer espouse the cause of enlightened liberalism. But surely, the actions of some unions do not condemn all unions. . . . Most university, college, and school librarians who are union members belong to the American Federation of Teachers, a group that did not support Wallace and which certainly has not been complacent over the last few years. Most public librarians who are union members belong to the American Federation of State, County and Municipal Employees. As one of the fastest growing unions in the country and as the principal union which has gone into the South and orga-

nized blacks—such as the Memphis garbage truck drivers—
AFSCME is not only compatible with social change and experiment, but it is one of the leaders in this area.

As strong, independent, professional organizations, library unions are characterized by two extremely important
elements. One of these is that they are democratic. This is
important for the professional. Those groups such as doctors
and lawyers, whose professional status no one questions, are
largely self-employed, setting their income and working conditions through two of the country's most powerful employee groups—the American Medical Association and the
American Bar Association. Some of the hallmarks of a professional, then, are his independence, his control over his
working situation, and his equality with all other members
of his profession. However, librarians work within an employee-employer relationship, which by its very structure
works against professionalism. The democratic structure of
a union, though, mitigates this problem because it enhances
the individual librarian's independence by placing him in a
situation where he is truly one among equals.

The second element which is characteristic of library
unions and is of considerable importance to library administrators is that, where there are unions, management and
workers alike have well-defined roles to play whenever a controversy arises. This is a very positive attribute of unions,
for it greatly lessens the kinds of confrontation that can take
place when there are no rules to govern a conflict. The history of unions has been in large part the establishment in
law of procedures to handle problems that would otherwise
escalate into serious conflict. This same structure also helps
divert a great deal of debilitating dissension into positive
research and action.

In conclusion, then, library unions help library administrators by:

1. Working independently for higher wages and better
   working conditions
2. Working independently for professional goals

3. Providing a forum from which the professional can speak to the public
4. Increasing the involvement of the individual librarian in the problems of his library
5. Providing a democratic structure within which all librarians are equals ...
6. Providing a framework within which problems can be solved

Unions of professional librarians exist to strengthen the individual libraries of their members and to strengthen the profession itself—at the local level, where the American Library Association is not effective. The direction that library unions are moving in is compatible with the direction of those . . . librarians who happen to be administrators. In addition, library unions will, without question, strengthen the ability of library administrators to improve ... [the] profession.

UNIONIZATION IS NOT INEVITABLE [5]

Labor union organization in libraries has become a foregone conclusion in some localities. Indeed, many people in the library profession have resigned themselves to the "inevitable" growth of the movement without so much as another look at the alternatives. The profession in general, has been relatively unconcerned with the activities of labor unions, even though these very activities may eventually place it in a position to be acted upon rather than in a position to act. The library profession should be fully aware of the implication of labor union representation before plunging headlong into a decision of "Should we or shouldn't we?" ...

Probably the most important aspect of developing an awareness of the unionization movement lies with individual

[5] From article by Keith M. Cottam, social science librarian, Brigham Young University, and instructor in library and information sciences. *Library Journal*. 93:4105-6. N. 1, '68. Reprinted from *Library Journal*, November 1, 1968, copyright © 1968 by the R. R. Bowker Co.

and personal responsibility. Each librarian should have the freedom and right to choose for himself what he believes to be right, but his choice should be made after a careful analysis of the facts before him.

A person unfamiliar with labor union organizations and professional associations may at first recognize general areas of common concern; but, on closer examination, several differences are very apparent. The improvement of employee welfare such as grievance procedures, working conditions, salaries, and retirement are common objectives of both groups; however, where the labor union, for all practical purposes, is concerned only with employee welfare, the professional association is concerned with the advancement of the entire profession. The professional association is partial to the interests of its members and has the background and knowledge to develop its own standards; standards of excellence in educating its members, with personnel and administrative relations and with service. Indeed, with more active support and interest in and by professional associations they could also develop the machinery for the enforcement of ethical conduct and direction, both for librarians and administrations.

The labor movement has been characterized as a movement of freedom; of people standing up on their own feet and organizing and carrying out the democratic process. If I thought for a moment that the rank and file member had a controlling interest in a labor union organization and really had an adequate voice in shaping its policies, and if I could be assured that those becoming involved in labor union activities were actually trying to improve their professional positions as much as they are looking for an easy way out of their present "predicaments," then perhaps I would revise my position on unionization for librarians and retreat to the relative "security" of union representation. I have yet to be convinced.

Labor unions have also been characterized as voluntary associations. It may be technically true that no person is physically forced to join a union, but it is equally true that in a unionized area a person must join a union if he wants to work and make a living. This is nothing but a form of coercion which demonstrates the hypocrisy of the idea that unions are voluntary associations.

Our individual and professional rights do not belong to organized labor groups. An individual librarian who associates himself with a labor union organization must immediately share his individual and professional responsibility with a group which is, in all probability, not partial to the aims and objectives of librarianship. An individual who associates himself with a labor union organization removes from his control several elements which are integral to the rights of the individual: his personal responsibility, freedom of initiative and incentive, and freedom for ambition above and beyond his associates. No amount of rationalization or action can justify this infringement simply because a majority approves. Labor leaders conveniently ignore the rights of the minority and the rights of the individual.

We are in the middle of a knowledge revolution. Education has come to mean power and money, and if anything in this country leads to these ends, people will put a lot of effort into it. The labor unions have no choice in the matter if they want to survive. With the decline of blue-collar workers the labor unions are looking for new areas of jurisdiction, and these new areas lie in places of education like library service. To put it bluntly, labor is looking for new areas to conquer, and these new conquests mean new members and new dues payers. The more money in the union coffers the more power and influence they are able to wield with the American public, certainly perpetuating a doctrine of "might makes right."

I do not deny the great tradition of trade unionism as a vital force in American society, of its contribution to the elevation of the working man, and of the security the movement has provided for thousands who would otherwise be under the cloak of poverty. Unions may be a necessity in some parts of our complex society, but they are by no means an end in themselves, nor do they hold the magic keys to success and security.

What, then, are the alternatives? To compete in our society a person must be educated, and librarians for the most part have completed at least seventeen years of school to qualify for the many positions available. Granted, we have a long way to go for a substantial minimum salary in many library situations, and I will be among the last to belittle increased and adequate monetary remuneration. With the education, and with consideration of the apparent voids of personnel in the library profession and the ease of mobility of our society, we have one alternative. A librarian will generally earn what he is willing to work for, and there are few limitations for librarians with sufficient education and with the wisdom of experience and ambition. The supply of librarians does not nearly satisfy the demand, and demand creates better opportunity for any librarian who will accept it. Naturally, this must be construed as nothing short of rugged individualism, a characteristic often forgotten in modern society and even subtly discouraged. For a librarian who desires a particular geographic location, it may be impossible to advance in the profession without some type of collective influence. The basic issue, then, must come down to what kind of collective influence the library profession should accept or develop.

Strong, vigorous professional associations at the local, state, and national levels, with backbone to defend the rights of librarians, offer what may be the most acceptable alternative for those who would prefer collective action. Professional associations by their very nature provide high motivation to work for the good of the members and the betterment of the profession. Professional associations at all levels are in a better position to provide and interpret accurate facts concerning the library profession. Local associations need not stand alone if state and national associations adequately organize their resources to provide the specific guidance and assistance needed. Their activities can lead not only to sound employee welfare, but also to sound library policy.

COLLECTIVE BARGAINING IN TVA [6]

The TVA Act of 1933 created an autonomous Federal Government corporation. It also provided that the corporation's board of directors "without regard to the provisions of Civil Service laws" would appoint and remove employees, fix their pay, and define their duties. This authority gave TVA a latitude in dealing with its employees which paralleled that given it to develop the resources of the Tennessee Valley. Therefore, circumstances favored the initiation of employee-management relationships which were to be unique in the Federal service of that day and many days to follow just as the time was also ripe to pioneer the concept of unified resource development.

The first board action of significance to employee-management relations came almost concurrently with the establishment of the agency. Facing the immediate task of building Norris and Wheeler Dams, the board decided to employ its own construction forces rather than use private contractors. For a considerable time, construction workers were the largest category of TVA employees, and a number of them were members of various American Federation of Labor building-trades unions. These unions, while hard hit by the Depression, served as a strong nucleus for the organization of our construction workers. The board's response to this situation came in July 1934 in the form of a resolution by which it recognized the right of employees to organize and join employee organizations and to bargain collectively. Thus, the TVA Board set a course on which the Federal service at large would not venture for another twenty-eight

[6] From "TVA Looks at Three Decades of Collective Bargaining," by Aubrey J. Wagner, chairman, Tennessee Valley Authority board of directors. *Industrial and Labor Relations Review*. 22:20-30. O. '68. Reprinted from the *Industrial and Labor Relations Review*, Vol. 22, No. 1, October 1968. Copyright © by Cornell University. All rights reserved.

years when Executive Order 10988 (Employee-Management Cooperation in the Federal Service) was issued. [See "Executive Order 10988," in Section V, below.]

The board's 1935 *Employee Relationship Policy* reaffirmed the principles of the 1934 resolution and provided a framework for development of relationships between the agency and organizations of employees. It set forth the principle of recognition of the representative of a majority of the employees in a defined bargaining unit as the exclusive representative of all the employees in such unit. It also envisaged the establishment of joint conferences between the recognized representatives of employees and of management for the purpose of systematic employee-management cooperation.

In effect, the *Employee Relationship Policy* of 1935 was an act of faith—an act of confidence—on the part of TVA management in TVA employees. . . .

Unions Are Recognized

Initially, TVA recognized individual AFL craft unions to represent employees in defined bargaining units. In 1937, these unions formed the Tennessee Valley Trades and Labor Council. In the same year, TVA recognized this council as the representative of these unions in collective bargaining for all blue-collar employees. The council and TVA entered into a formal agreement in 1940. Today, the council represents fifteen craft unions affiliated with the AFL-CIO and one unaffiliated union each of which has recognition as the exclusive representative of the employees in its craft. In June 1968, the agreement covered 5,000 operating and maintenance employees and 7,000 construction workers. In December 1967, TVA and the council held their thirty-third annual wage negotiations.

White-collar employees organized at a slower pace. By 1943, five AFL unions and two independent employee organizations had been recognized by TVA as exclusive representatives of various groups of white-collar employees on matters affecting only the employees in those groups. The AFL unions organized themselves into a council, which in turn joined with the two independent unions to form the Salary Policy Employee Panel. The panel was recognized by TVA in 1943 as the bargaining representative for white-collar employees on matters affecting these employees generally. A formal agreement between the panel and TVA came into being in 1950. Today, the panel consists of three AFL-CIO-affiliated unions and two independent associations. These organizations represent some 6,000 of the 7,500 white-collar positions. Most of the remaining 1,500 white-collar positions are either managerial or so closely related to managerial functions that they are not included under the contract. TVA and the panel held their seventeenth annual salary negotiations in the spring of 1968.

All negotiations are conducted either with the council or the panel, each of which, as noted above, has a formal agreement with TVA. The agreements apply to all the employees in the bargaining units represented by the recognized unions which are part of either the council or the panel. However, within the framework of each formal agreement, TVA will discuss and work cooperatively with any of the constituent unions of either body on matters affecting only the employees in the defined bargaining unit represented by that union. Such matters are almost entirely in the realm of contract administration. For example, matters such as leave schedules, questions about overtime distribution, details of operation of formal joint training programs, or physical working conditions (e.g., lighting, ventilation, etc.) involving employees in a work group consisting exclusively of employees represented by one union are worked out on an informal basis with that union. Also, a grievance is normally handled by an individual union rather than by the panel or the council. . . . This arrangement allows for equitable treatment of all employees without imposing uniformity which restricts the handling of problems peculiar to one group of employees.

The formal contracts signed in 1940 and 1950 marked an end and a beginning for union-management relationships in TVA. In those years, the respective parties to each contract succeeded in jointly creating a permanent framework for their relationships. Because this framework proved durable, both contracts were still in effect in 1962 and thus were not affected by Executive Order 10988. Their comprehensive coverage of pay and fringe benefits, hours of work, and working conditions still sets them apart from agreements negotiated under the order. But more than a durable framework was required to keep these documents alive. TVA, the council, and the panel treated these contracts not simply as documents but as tools—tools to meet the everchanging needs of TVA and of the employee organizations. This approach to the contracts has resulted in innumerable and significant revisions in the agreements since their formal beginnings.

ON THE FRINGE: NURSES [7]

It has been . . . [many] years since legislation was first passed to encourage employees in private employment in the establishment of collective bargaining relationships. . . . [Since 1962] employees in the Federal Government and in many state jurisdictions have been given similar encouragement. Yet, many groups of workers still remain outside the area of protected collective bargaining activity. In the give-and-take of legislative enactment, some groups do not press their interests, and others are considered too insignificant to receive careful consideration. This is perhaps an inevitable part of the legislative process, but it also suggests that when it becomes apparent that inequities have been allowed to develop new legislation must be created to eliminate them.

Nurses employed in nonprofit hospitals constitute one group whose situation merits careful consideration. Their

[7] From "Nurses, Collective Bargaining and Labor Legislation," by Archie Kleingartner, associate professor of industrial relations and vice chairman, Graduate School of Business Administration, University of California, Los Angeles. *Labor Law Journal.* 18:236-45. Ap. '67. Reprinted by permission.

position under existing labor legislation seems strangely archaic when we consider the large numbers involved and events indicative of the determination of nurses to promote collective bargaining with hospitals. The exclusion of all nonprofit hospitals from Taft-Hartley Act coverage, and the pattern this has set for other jurisdictions, is one of the main obstacles to the achievement of their collective bargaining objectives.

For all practical purposes, to speak of nurses and collective bargaining is to speak of the activities of the American Nurses' Association and its state affiliates. While the ANA can claim as members only about 28 per cent of all employed nurses, there exists at the same time no significant organizational opposition within nursing to the ANA. In other salaried professions, teaching for one, there exists sharp rivalry for members and representation rights. The ANA is the single dominant organization representing nurses in all of their job and professional problems. It draws no distinction between its functions as a professional association and as an economic institution.

The basic collective policy of the ANA dates back to 1946, when its convention adopted an "Economic Security Program."

The American Nurses' Association believes that the several state and district nurses' associations are qualified to act and should act as the exclusive agents of their respective memberships in the important fields of economic security and collective bargaining. The Association commends the excellent progress already made and urges all state and district nurses' associations to push such a program vigorously and expeditiously.

It is of general interest that the ANA, unlike some other professional organizations, not only proposed a collective bargaining program but also called it collective bargaining. It still does. The ANA itself does no bargaining; its state affiliates are charged with this responsibility. All of them have adopted bargaining programs along the lines suggested by the parent ANA. These include seeking recognition as the exclusive bargaining agent, after the manner of trade unions generally, and negotiating written agreements with employers.

The ANA's 1946 statement on economic security called for collective action on such traditional collective bargaining items as a forty-hour work week, higher minimum salaries and improved fringe benefits, as well as on the more uniquely professional matters such as participation by nurses in the planning and administration of nursing services.

The goal of the ANA in 1946, to set up a bona fide collective bargaining apparatus, was further evidenced in 1948 when it called upon its state affiliates to refrain from entering into "joint programs for economic security" with state hospital associations (federations of hospital employers) on the ground that this would open the whole program to charges of company unionism.

The ANA sees no conflict between the ethical codes of the nursing profession and collective bargaining. As a matter of fact, it views collective bargaining as an ethical imperative to help nursing achieve true professional status. . . .

How do rank-and-file nurses view collective bargaining? Unfortunately there is no precise way to measure their interest. The percentage of nurses who join the ANA is probably not a good index, because nurses decide to join or not join for a variety of reasons not related to collective bargaining. In almost every issue of the *American Journal of Nursing*, the official publication of the ANA, the question of collective bargaining is treated. Letters to the editor of this journal generally stress the need for more militancy and greater emphasis on bargaining.

Recent activity by rank-and-file nurses provides more impressive evidence. The summer of 1966 demonstrated in California and elsewhere the deep dissatisfaction of many nurses with their conditions and their readiness to support collective action, even if unable to translate this into collective bargaining. "It's taken one hundred years to get the starch out of the uniforms and into our spines," is how one nurse reportedly described what is happening. In San Francisco 2,000 registered nurses out of 3,700 employed in 33 different hospitals submitted their resignations because of the failure of the hospital association and the California Nurses' Association (CNA) to agree on wages. A compromise was reached short of an actual walkout, but many nurses felt that their negotiators should have held out for more money. Barely one half of the over 1,000 nurses who attended the ratification meeting supported the agreement. . . .

In the face of this militancy, hospital associations sought to maintain a united front and were severely critical of those hospitals unilaterally giving salary increases above the agreed-upon rate. At the same time unions were putting out feelers to test the depth of the nurses' dissatisfaction with existing conditions. The large Los Angeles local of the Retail Clerks Union established the Registered Nurses Guild of Southern California to organize nurses. Calling for a union approach to nurses' problems, the local criticized the efforts of the California Nurses' Association. . . .

The Status of Nurses Under
Collective Bargaining Legislation

The central dilemma of the nurses is that Section 2 (2) of the Taft-Hartley Act excludes from coverage employees of hospitals operated on a nonprofit basis. Thus these employees are prohibited from requesting representation elections, filing unfair labor practice charges with the NLRB [National Labor Relations Board], and from having recourse to any Federal agencies. The ANA and its state affiliates strongly endorse the necessity and propriety of these rights. The ANA views the exemption provision as being discriminatory and restrictive. . . .

Only three states—Oregon, Massachusetts and New York —have laws with enforcement provisions which specifically provide for bargaining between nonprofit hospitals and nurses. In some states legislation has been introduced but without final approval. . . .

Nursing is a good example of a profession which is greatly in need of the types of benefits that have been derived from bargaining, where substantial interest in bargaining exists, and where employers have generally been unwilling to engage in meaningful bargaining without an element of coercion. It does not seem inappropriate to suggest that the Federal Congress and state legislatures take a careful look at whether the best interests of the community are being served by the continued exclusion of nonprofit hospitals from collective bargaining legislation.

III. TEACHERS AND COLLECTIVE BARGAINING

EDITOR'S INTRODUCTION

Affecting as it does every child and every parent of school-age children, a strike of teachers draws more widespread community attention than virtually any other type of work stoppage, public or private. The collective bargaining action of educators (teachers at all levels and administrators as well) has caused an almost total destruction of the past stereotype of the teacher as a genteel servant of the local board of education.

Walter Goodman in the first selection examines the background of teachers' strikes. Professor Robert L. Walter, a former school superintendent, suggests that there are other methods by which teachers may improve their status and increase their participation in policy making. Philip A. Grant, Jr., discusses unionism at the college and university level; an American Federation of Teachers official, Mr. Grant tells his story from the union point of view and provides insight into the methods and aims of public employee unions. The "AAUP Position on Strikes" is a carefully drafted position statement for college professors on the question of their participation in work stoppages. Finally, "Should Teachers Have the Right to Strike?" examines the pros and cons of this emotion-filled question.

WHY TEACHERS ARE STRIKING [1]

A week after the opening of school in Rapid City, South Dakota . . . [in 1968], more than 400 of the city's 500 classroom teachers announced their withdrawal of services. In

[1] From an article by Walter Goodman, contributing editor. *Redbook.* 132: 67+. Mr. '69. Copyright © 1969 The McCall Publishing Company. Reprinted by permission.

ordinary English, they were striking—an unprecedented action in the conservative bastion of Rapid City, and one that startled school board members, principals, parents, children and, as a matter of fact, the teachers themselves.

The Rapid City walkout was one of a rash of strikes . . . that, to the growing consternation of parents everywhere, shut down scores of schools serving thousands of children around the country. Schools were affected in parts of Michigan, Connecticut, Illinois, Indiana, Tennessee, and New York, as well as in South Dakota. Shutdowns were narrowly —and perhaps only temporarily—averted in such major cities as Philadelphia and St. Louis. The previous school year saw major disputes flare in New York City and in Detroit. In Florida teachers staged their first statewide walkout, the biggest up to that time, involving 1,241,000 children. And despite widespread prohibitions against such strikes, these promise to be only the beginning. The talk now in teachers' circles is of a possible *nationwide* walkout.

A generation ago strikes by teachers were virtually unheard of; a decade ago they were rare; today they are a troubling part of school life. To understand why this is so, we have to understand something of what has been happening in recent years to the teaching profession, to public education and indeed to the temper of the nation as a whole.

It was the odd combination of a spiraling birth rate in America and Soviet successes in outer space that turned the nation's attention to its schools in the 1950s. American education, particularly in science, was not keeping up with that of the Soviet Union. Furthermore, it was not making provisions for the ever-increasing numbers of students. Where there had been smug satisfaction, suddenly there was near panic, with flurries of action on every level from the local PTA to the Federal Government, which poured millions of dollars into the school system.

One result of this intensive and expensive concern was a dramatic transformation of the image and the nature of the schoolteacher. For decades the teaching profession, besides attracting the dedicated but rare teacher, had been a haven for the girl occupying her time before marriage, the married woman making a contribution to the family income and the middle-aged spinster whom marriage had, alas, eluded. Suddenly, with the opening of new opportunities, teaching began to attract a markedly different kind of college student. The women now tended to be lured by the challenge of the work, not only by the prospect of a sinecure. More notably, men began to enter the profession in large numbers. Today about a third of the country's teachers are male; they make up a majority in our secondary schools and form a leadership cadre in school districts everywhere.

The effects can be seen in the Rapid City strike. The head of Rapid City's teachers' organization is a male math teacher, aged twenty-nine. The eighty-three teachers who did not join the walkout were nearly all women and nearly all in elementary schools, where a principal's relationship with his teachers is usually close and sometimes paternal. But the junior high and high schools, where male teachers were in the majority, were shut down completely....

National figures indicate that the teacher has in fact been getting more money. In 1947 the average pay in our public schools was $2,254 a year. In 1957 it was $4,350. And in 1967 it was up to $7,119—higher in the Far West, substantially lower in the Southeast. The teacher's average money gain over the past decade comes to about 5 per cent a year, more than the gains of most industrial and white-collar workers, though teachers have yet to catch up to miners, steelworkers, plumbers and electricians. ...

Although money is the spur for most teachers' strikes, the impulses behind them often go deeper than dollars and cents. In the eighteen months before the Rapid City strike, starting pay in the school system had risen from a low $4,500 to $5,300, and a further rise was in sight. The average salary was on a par with most of the country. But there was widespread discontent among the teachers over the way they had been treated for years by the city's school administrators and board of education: "They never dealt with us as equals; they gave us a pat on the head and told us to run along. Even today we're being dictated to by people who know nothing at all about teaching. That's what burns me up."

Yet for all their dissatisfactions, it has not been easy for teachers to adopt militant tactics. Even the angriest teacher in Rapid City was not entirely comfortable in the role of disrupter of the established order. "I voted twice against striking," said a seventh-grade teacher, "because I didn't want us to be confused with a labor union. But when the issue came to a head, I couldn't desert my colleagues." Determined though a majority of the teachers were to hold firm against the school board, most shared a reluctance to behave like ordinary unionists. They refused to picket the elementary schools that remained open, despite the recommendation of advisers from the National Education Association. . . .

Whatever their personal feelings or the feelings of their students, however, teachers are learning that in a labor dispute there is no more effective show of strength than an all-out strike. When Detroit's eleven thousand teachers returned to their classrooms after a two-week walkout in the fall of 1967, they had won a raise of $850 a year. Such results help to explain the recent poll showing that nearly seven out of ten teachers now believe that strikes are justified. . . .

Teacher militancy won its first significant victory in 1961, when a local of the AFL-CIO's American Federation of Teachers (AFT) defeated the old-line National Education Association to become bargaining representative for New York City's 55,000 teachers. The NEA, with more than a million dues-paying members, had traditionally frowned upon strikes and concentrated its efforts on research directed at maintaining professional standards. . . .

Unlike the NEA, the AFT is a labor union first and foremost, unmistakably in existence to get more of the good things of life for its members. With that clear program, following its victory . . . [in 1961] in New York City it took over from the NEA in such cities as Chicago, Philadelphia, Detroit, Cleveland, Boston, Baltimore and Pittsburgh, and in so doing has forced the NEA to compete. The NEA gave an earnest of its new militancy in February 1968, when it paid out $2 million to wage the angry statewide strike in Florida, where some twenty thousand teachers stayed out of the classrooms for nearly three weeks. And it was the NEA's Rapid City affiliate that called the strike in that city, with full backing from the national body.

The lesson that teachers have been taught by the experience of the 1960s is a simple one: Militancy works. As former NEA President Elizabeth Koontz [now director of the Women's Bureau of the United States Department of Labor] declares: "The militancy of teachers will not go away; no amount of wishing will make it so." Because of AFT bargaining, starting salaries of Chicago's teachers rose from $5,500 in 1967 to $6,560 in 1968, and as a result of last fall's strike in East St. Louis, Illinois, which kept 24,000 students out of school for four weeks, starting salaries jumped from $6,250 to $8,000. . . .

It is the working of the economic system that has set parents and teachers on a collision course. Parents in suburban communities around the country, where school taxes have been going up year after year with no end in sight, are famous for demanding the best teachers and the best facilities for their children—that's a major reason for their move to the suburbs, after all—yet even they have been showing increasing resistance to paying the endlessly rising school bills. Without such rises, of course, teachers' demands cannot be met, yet in many towns school budgets have been voted down.

The most dramatic clash between teachers and parents, however, has come not in our prosperous suburbs but in the impoverished black ghettos of New York City. The opening of all city schools was disrupted . . . [in the fall of 1968] after some community residents in the largely black Ocean Hill-Brownsville area of Brooklyn defied the city's board of education and refused to let a number of white teachers and administrators resume their posts in the neighborhood's schools. The United Federation of Teachers (the AFT local), charging that the new decentralization plan for New York's schools would lead to other instances of arbitrary transfers and so jeopardize the status of all teachers, called a much-criticized series of citywide strikes.

Here, amid threats of violence and bitter racial and religious recriminations, community militancy and teacher militancy met head-on. For the recently established experimental local governing board of Ocean Hill-Brownsville, the clash was proof that the control black people are seeking over the running of their own communities will not be granted easily. For the union leadership, the prospect of school decentralization was seen as a threat to its own hard-won power, and a decision was made to turn Ocean Hill-Brownsville into a test case, despite the effects of a lengthy school strike on a million New York City children.

The legacy of this clash has been to deepen the gulf between black parents and white teachers in New York, to cast doubt on the ability of local boards to protect the rights of all teachers in the face of pressure from black militants in their communities and to make suspect the claims of white teachers that they are interested primarily in their students' welfare rather than in their own vested interests. . . .

The fiery emotions loosed in the course of this dispute, which reflects many of the seemingly insoluble problems that beset our cities, make a reconciliation unlikely in the near future. Yet one need not be an incorrigible optimist to see a glimmer of hope that ghetto parents may have less cause for criticism of their children's teachers tomorrow than they had yesterday. It may be a sign of things to come that a small but not insignificant minority of New York's white teachers, particularly younger ones, broke with their union leadership last fall and continued to teach in strikebound schools.

AFT president David Selden thinks that the real fault of the teachers over the years has not been lack of interest but lack of militancy. There is something to this. The new militancy of the new breed of teacher is a response to the times; it evidences a growing, if belated, realization that there is no longer any way of separating a teacher's welfare from the welfare of the school system where he works and the children in his care. One of the teachers' demands in the 1967 New York City strike was retention of the More Effective Schools Program for slum children, which some city officials wanted to abolish. A major issue in the Florida walkout was the quality of the school buildings and instructional materials. "In some schools there were no desks," one new teacher said indignantly, "and books were out of date. I saw textbooks that had sections on the *possibility* of sending a rocket into space."

A high-school teacher in Rapid City, whose schedule had her conducting five classes in a row in five different rooms before her midday break, reports: "I was teaching English without a dictionary and social studies without a globe. I had no desk of my own and had to scrounge around for textbooks." . . .

Turning to suburban districts, where taxpayers are showing signs of rebelling against constantly rising school expenses, Selden suggests that it is time to reevaluate our traditional method of paying for schools by taxing homeowners.

Maybe, if we want to encourage homeownership, it's unsound to raise property taxes above their present level. I think education is going to have to be financed more and more out of general state and Federal revenues, out of income taxes and sales taxes. If people complain about that, they ought to understand that they are paying for bad education every time there is a riot or an outbreak of crime, so they might as well pay for good education.

Selden is not troubled by the fear often voiced by conservative congressmen that Federal interference must follow Federal funds.

We're concerned about the Federal Government's *not* coming in. At present, there are vast regional differences in the quality of schools that are directly related to the wealth of a particular state or district. Only the Federal Government can compensate for these differences. We want nationwide standards of educational decency.

It remains to be seen whether the teaching profession will live up to its protestations of concern for educational quality or will merely broadcast slogans about quality to justify its own demands for more money. It is ingenuous to believe that teachers, any more than members of any other trade or profession, are eager to sacrifice their self-interest to the larger interests of the community. Nonetheless, there are voices from younger teachers and from students now in training that bear witness to a desire to show much greater social responsibility. . . .

America's teachers are proving that they have power and are capable of using it to advance their own interests. But involved as they are in so sensitive and critical an enterprise as helping to raise tomorrow's citizens, self-interest is clearly not enough. What parents are asking is how the new militancy is going to affect them, their community, their children. "I would hope," says young Mel Myler [of the Student NEA], "that in the very near future parents will be joining teachers on the picket line." Whether parents do so will depend on whether they are convinced that teachers are really matching their efforts in behalf of their own well-being with efforts in behalf of their students.

AN ALTERNATIVE TO COLLECTIVE BARGAINING: FACULTY PARTICIPATION IN POLICY MAKING [2]

Can a method be devised which will satisfy faculty demands for a share in decision making without resorting to collective bargaining? Can the legitimate interests of school boards, teachers, administrators, pupils and the general pub-

[2] From "An Alternative to Collective Bargaining," by Dr. Robert L. Walter, associate professor of educational administration, Temple University, and former superintendent, Indian Hill School District, Cincinnati. *American School Board Journal.* 155:26-7. Mr. '68. Copyright by the National School Boards Association. Reprinted by permission.

lic be protected in some form of interaction without adopting the strategies and procedures of industrial negotiations?

Experience illustrates why industrial negotiation methods are not appropriate for public education. Unreasonable demands, weeks of fruitless maneuvering, last-minute, tension-filled attempts to reach a compromise—these are the strategies employed regularly in industrial bargaining to institutionalize and control conflict and to develop a means of shared decision making.

Teachers today expect and will continue to demand a more effective voice in the determination of school policy. If improved ways of achieving this aim are not found, many will opt for industrial-type negotiations *and* the attending chaos.

Seven years ago the Indian Hill School District in suburban Cincinnati rejected both the ritualized combat of collective bargaining and school board paternalism by developing a new method of faculty participation in the formation of policy. Called shared policy initiation, the concept focuses faculty participation upon identification of need and origination of policy to meet that need.

The organizational structure in Indian Hill is provided by a standing personnel advisory committee composed of four members of the faculty, three laymen from the community, a member of the school board and the superintendent. This group is charged by the board of education with the responsibility of doing the basic research and development of personnel policy formation. The widest possible definition of personnel is given so that any matter of direct concern to any employee of the district is within the mandate.

Every member sits on the committee as an individual, not as the representative of any group. He brings his knowledge, experience and judgment to bear to ensure that the board makes decisions in light of the best possible study. Responsibility is to the welfare of students attending the schools. Partially because the board perceives this group as free from outside pressure, no recommendation of the committee has been rejected or even modified substantially by the board in seven years of experience with shared policy initiation.

How can a board of education release its policy-making authority to a committee? The answer in Indian Hill is that the board has released no authority. The strictest kind of control exists over the actions of the committee. And committee members realize that their opportunity to continue to be the effective, if not the legal, policy-making agency rests solely upon continued evidence of responsibility and restraint in their recommendations.

Staunch advocates of collective bargaining strategies may say the committee is a front for the board, that its puppet status is proved by the fact that none of its recommendations have been turned down.

Two facts refute this argument. In the first place, a puppet role presumes that decisions are reached *a priori* by the board and then given respectability by the committee. This is simply not the case in Indian Hill. Throughout the full experience of the committee, consideration of personnel issues has been initiated by the committee and recommendations, together with supportive evidence, forwarded to the board. The degree of acceptance by the board has resulted from the quality of the recommendations themselves.

The second rebuttal to the charge of "company union" is the condition of restraint imposed upon the board. The personnel advisory committee can be effective as an alternate to collective bargaining only as long as the faculty believes it is not a front organization.

So, a form of checks and balances has evolved during the seven-year period. The faculty is restrained from irresponsibility in order to keep intact a system which has given teachers a great deal of decision-making power. The board of education is restrained from arbitrary actions through its realization that these decisions, based upon careful fact finding, are good for the schools.

In shared policy initiation, the superintendent of schools
is able to play the kind of policy formation role for which he
has been trained and is accustomed. Where collective bargaining exists, he is torn between abandonment of his professional colleagues in order to represent the board or shun-
ning the action altogether and sitting on the sidelines while
faculty and board contend.

Shared policy initiation permits the superintendent to
serve the committee as a source of information and professional guidance. This is the role recommended for him in the
decision-making activities of the board. Since the committee
serves as a surrogate for the board, the superintendent's role
is unchanged in a sense.

In collective bargaining, the superintendent faces a Hob-
son's choice. Shall he appear on the teachers' side of the table,
aligned with his professional colleagues? If so, he opposes
those who employed him as their professional counselor and
chief executive officer. Or, does he go the other way and combat the faculty to which he necessarily must provide professional leadership?

Shared policy initiation leaves the superintendent a realistic opportunity to save his professional manhood without
divorcing himself from either of the two reference groups
with whom he must work. He, too, has self-interest in keeping the checks and balances operative.

In Indian Hill, members of the personnel advisory committee have been carefully chosen to insure the expertise and
judgment necessary to continue the high quality of recommendations which have come from the committee. Lay members have been invited to participate by the president of the
board of education.

Responsibility for choosing faculty members resides with
the superintendent. In practice, however, this prerogative has
been delegated to the president of the Classroom Teachers'
Association.

Such an arrangement guards against charges of administration domination through the selection of toadies. Yet, this

practice has been the source of the most difficult problems in making the shared policy concept work.

Although faculty members sit on the committee as individuals chosen to assist the board of education to make wise policy, their *de facto* appointment by the president of the Classroom Teachers' Association has led to a persistent misconception by some association members that the association is represented on the committee. This difficulty in role perception becomes serious when members of the teachers' association propose that their representatives to the advisory committee be instructed in certain ways. Involved explanations are then necessary, and confusion has frequently resulted. Charges have been leveled that the association, as an association, is blocked from participation.

So far, these situations have been satisfactorily resolved. Competing teacher organizations, however, have created a climate in favor of more association power to adequately protect teacher interests. In this atmosphere, attention must be given to ways in which more direct association participation may be provided.

No claim is made by those who have participated in the Indian Hill experience that it is unique. Faculty, administration and board attempts to work cooperatively have been widespread for years. What does seem of interest in this experience is that the shared policy system was designed to provide an alternative to the movement toward formal collective bargaining in public schools.

Indian Hill, like many districts, previously had given faculty members an opportunity to be heard on school matters. From the time of its inception, however, the shared policy plan has fixed the responsibility for identifying potential problems and proposing acceptable solutions to a group having a plurality of faculty.

No claim is made that shared policy initiation is necessarily exportable to other situations. Circumstances in every district are bound to be sufficiently different that no single solution to the problem of effective decision making on the part of the board is apt to be found. What is claimed, however, is that . . . experience in this district has established evidence not lightly to be dismissed that an alternative to formal collective bargaining can be developed in public education.

Success in Indian Hill gives a basis for hope that those who teach and those who administer the public's schools may not need to face the conflict, recriminations and loss of productivity which so frequently are the price of more primitive attempts at shared decision making.

UNIONISM IN HIGHER EDUCATION [3]

Thus far, the progress of unionization among college faculties has been quite modest. A total of 104 locals have been chartered and approximately fourteen thousand professors have affiliated with AFT [the American Federation of Teachers (AFL-CIO)]. In four states, New York, Illinois, Michigan, and Rhode Island, the AFT has been acknowledged as the official bargaining agent at particular institutions of higher learning. There has been steadily accelerating union activity in California, Oregon, Washington, and New Jersey. . . . Interestingly, the recorded successes of the AFT in higher education have been confined largely to public rather than private institutions.

Until recently, the only national organization of college faculty members has been the American Association of University Professors (AAUP). Although the AAUP has maintained an admirable position on academic freedom, a thorough analysis of its policies reveals that the organization has been generally acquiescent during the half century of its existence. Indeed the apparent reluctance of the AAUP to assert itself more vigorously as a vital force in American higher education is perhaps the most convincing argument in

    [3] From article by Philip A. Grant, Jr., associate professor of history, University of Dayton, and secretary, University of Dayton Federation of Teachers, Local 1850, American Federation of Teachers (AFL-CIO). *Labor Today*. 7:24-8. Fall '68. Reprinted by permission.

favor of the AFT as a dynamic alternative. [See "AAUP Position on Strikes," in this section, below.]

At the present time the need is critical for the college professor to achieve progress in the three essential areas of compensation, tenure, and academic conditions. . . .

Merely to deplore the multitude of problems plaguing contemporary American higher education is insufficient. The need is urgent for college professors to consider the merits of the programs advocated by the recently established College Department of the AFT.

First of all, the AFT's College Department has initiated a publicity campaign dramatizing the complex problems confronting the nation's professors. . . .

Secondly, the College Department has outlined the AFT's priority objectives clearly and positively. The AFT unequivocally insists upon the maximum degree of academic freedom and complete freedom of association for both professors and students. This of necessity involves unrestricted freedom to teach, engage in research, and publish in accordance with professional standards. Conversely, the AFT opposes loyalty and disclaimer oaths. As for compensation, the AFT advocates steady economic advancement with the years of professional experience, a basic salary ranging from $10,000 to $30,000 in mandatory, equal, annual increments, and a public salary schedule for all college professors. The AFT urges automatic sabbaticals after each six years of service, a system of retirement allowances to assure annual benefits at no less than half pay of the highest year of salary, and unlimited sick pay subject to medical prognosis. The election of departmental chairmen and the limitation of nine teaching hours on the undergraduate level and six hours on the graduate level have also been endorsed by the AFT. Of paramount importance, the AFT stand on tenure is forthright and unmistakable, inasmuch as the AFT pledges immediate and unconditional support for any professor dismissed without exhaustive due process. Obviously, such dismissals are highly improbable at institutions organized by the AFT, because

AFT contracts specifically define all justifiable causes for dismissal as well as norms for promotion. In the possible event of contract violations, however, the AFT promises appropriate legal action and, if the circumstances warrant, will not hesitate to strike. The AFT, of course, emphasizes that its priority objectives are entirely consistent with both the inherent dignity of the academic community and the fundamental principles of the AFL-CIO.

Thirdly, the AFT is engaged in a concerted effort to secure the enactment of salutary labor legislation in the various states. Not only is the AFT striving to guarantee the right to bargain collectively at state universities, but also to extend this right to private institutions. It is appalling that so few of the fifty states have statutes protecting the rights of professors at either public or private institutions.

It is certain that the AFT will accelerate its organizing activities at American colleges and universities in the near future. Admittedly a nationwide organizing drive will be a formidable and expensive task. . . .

The foremost problem facing the AFT is undoubtedly the high financial cost of mobilizing to meet the numerous challenges of American higher education. The expenses of establishing a chain of regional offices throughout the nation and retaining attorneys on a full time basis are indeed substantial. In times of emergency, of course, the AFT can appeal to the AFL-CIO . . . [Council] for Scientific, Professional, and Cultural Employees (SPACE) and to numerous other labor organizations for legal assistance and financial support.

Another major problem may be the AFT's difficulty in recruiting large numbers of professors at the nation's prestigious institutions. With few exceptions these professors are being amply compensated for their academic services and have relatively insignificant grievances. Even if such distinguished academicians believe that unionization is unnecessary at their own universities, the AFT is anxious to cultivate their sympathy and assistance, inasmuch as they would lend valuable prestige and moral support to the AFT's quest to improve conditions for their less fortunate colleagues at other institutions.

While the AFT advocates boycotts and strikes only as last resorts, they have been and probably will continue to be necessary at various times and places. . . . [Two] AFT strikes of consequence have been the ones conducted at the city college system in Chicago [and] Lake Michigan College in Benton Harbor, Michigan. . . . If the results of these . . . strikes are in any way indicative of future trends in American higher education, the AFT has reason for genuine encouragement.

The December 1966 strike at the eight campuses of the Chicago City College lasted three days and was supported by approximately 650 professors. After more than two hundred hours of collective bargaining, the dispute was brought to an honorable conclusion with the signing of a two-year contract between the local educational authorities and the Cook County College Teachers Union, Local 1600 of the AFT. Local 1600 gained a substantial reduction in class contact hours, a three-year tenure policy, a $500 salary increase for each professor as well as $300 in additional fringe benefits, and an enlarged role for the faculty in hiring of new professors, renewal of individual contracts, and selection of departmental chairmen. . . .

At Lake Michigan College the AFT strike extended six weeks and was participated in by forty-nine professors. The strike was finally resolved on November 17, 1967, by a three-man arbitration panel. The terms of the settlement included a minimum salary increase of $1,000 for each professor, a two-week reduction in the length of the academic year, a limitation of both lecture hours and extracurricular duties, guaranteed sick leave, and a provision for the binding arbitration of future grievances. Although Lake Michigan College is a relatively young institution with a somewhat modest enrollment of two thousand students, the contract negotiated by the AFT will in all likelihood have a considerable effect on other colleges and universities in Michigan. . . .

Future Measures

As for the future, three measures seem indispensable to enhance the prospects of a prolonged academic strike. First of all, there must be a total boycott of the institution in question by all AFL-CIO unions. Secondly, there must be a sufficiently large strike fund available for the material needs of the affected professors. Thirdly, there must be well-coordinated efforts to alert government officials and accrediting agencies of discriminatory labor practices and academic irregularities disrupting the normal operations. . . .

The college professor must be reminded that bar associations and medical societies have been able to prescribe standards and control entry into the profession. Conversely, he must acknowledge how grossly inadequate have been the alternatives for himself and his colleagues in higher education. The college professor is an employee professional who does not determine his own fee and without strong organization will continue to be highly vulnerable. The need is pressing for systematic efforts on the campus to defend the individual professor, to investigate grievances, and to strive for a functioning faculty voice in academic conditions and compensation. The harsh reality is that administrators have unilaterally decreed the conditions under which the profession is practiced. Regretfully, the college professor has been reduced to a mere commodity in the academic marketplace.

If conditions are to be improved, the college professor must assume primary responsibility for their improvement. Alone the professor is totally without influence. Only if he unites with other professors in an organization genuinely committed to the welfare of the faculty at all times will substantial improvement be forthcoming. Through the AFT the vocation of college teaching can reach true professional status. The present time is probably the most critical period in the history of American higher education. The college professor must react positively to the challenges of the times to attain a much greater measure of professional self-determination. Indeed he must respectfully consider both the merits of the policies advocated by the AFT and the potential of the AFT as a constructive force in the quest for academic excellence.

AAUP POSITION ON STRIKES [4]

The American Association of University Professors is deeply committed to the proposition that faculty members in higher education are officers of their colleges and universities. They are not merely employees. They have direct professional obligations to their students, their colleagues, and their disciplines. Because of their professional competence, they have primary responsibility for central educational decisions; they share in the selection of presidents and deans; and their judgment should come first in the determination of membership in the faculty. Where these principles (which are more fully stated in the 1966 *Statement on Government of Colleges and Universities*) are not accepted in their entirety, the Association will continue to press for their realization. We believe that these principles of shared authority and responsibility render the strike inappropriate as a mechanism for the resolution of most conflicts within higher education.

But it does not follow from these considerations of self-restraint that professors should be under any legal disability to withhold their services, except when such restrictions are imposed equally on other citizens. Furthermore, situations may arise affecting a college or university which so flagrantly violate academic freedom (of students as well as of faculty) or the principles of academic government, and which are so resistant to rational methods of discussion, persuasion, and conciliation, that faculty members may feel impelled to express their condemnation by withholding their services, either individually or in concert with others. It should be assumed that faculty members will exercise their right to strike only if they believe that another component of the in-

[4] "Statement on Faculty Participation in Strikes," excerpted from article "Faculty Participation in Strikes." *AAUP (American Association of University Professors) Bulletin.* 54:155-9. Summer '68. Reprinted by permission.

stitution (or a controlling agency of government, such as a legislature or governor) is inflexibly bent on a course which undermines an essential element of the educational process.

Participation in a strike does not by itself constitute grounds for dismissal or for other sanctions against faculty members. Moreover, if dismissal of a faculty member is proposed on this, as on any other ground encompassed by the 1940 *Statement of Principles on Academic Freedom and Tenure,* the proceedings must satisfy the requirements of the 1958 *Statement of Procedural Standards in Faculty Dismissal Proceedings.* The Association will continue to protect the interests of members of the profession who are singled out for punishment on grounds which are inadequate or unacceptable, or who are not offered all the protection demanded by the requisites of due process.

SHOULD TEACHERS HAVE THE RIGHT TO STRIKE? [5]

Elizabeth D. Koontz, past president of the National Education Association and now director of the Women's Bureau of the Department of Labor, says:

The public owns the schools. It has the right, responsibility and obligation to provide the working conditions, the staff and the funds that the teacher needs to perform his task of teaching the community's children. If legislatures, school boards, communities and parents turn their backs on overworked, underpaid teachers and disgraceful teaching conditions, who then is left to speak out for the children? Teachers must organize, agitate, and, when all else fails, withdraw their services for as long as necessary to force the community into action.

William F. Condon, former New York State senator and cosponsor of the state's law prohibiting strikes by public employees, says:

No civil servants, including teachers, have the right to strike. When teachers take their jobs they know what the salary scale is,

[5] From article "The GH Poll: Should Teachers Have the Right to Strike?" *Good Housekeeping.* 168:12+. Ap. '69. Condensed by permission from the April, 1969, issue of *Good Housekeeping* Magazine. © 1969 by the Hearst Corporation.

what promotions can be expected, what pensions and other benefits are offered. The public, which pays the bill through taxes, has
the right to expect that such public employees as teachers, policemen, firemen and prison guards will stay on their jobs. If there
are grievances, regular bargaining channels are available, and if
these procedures do not work, teachers should ask the mayor or
the governor to appoint a special panel to settle the dispute.

When members of the GH [*Good Housekeeping*] Consumer Panel vote on the right of the nation's teachers to go
on strike, the results aren't even close.

Three out of four panelists declare, "No strike." And
nearly nine out of ten further insist, "No picketing." Only
13.4 per cent of those polled have actually experienced a
strike of teachers in their own community, but news of New
York City's ten-week strike . . . [in the fall of 1968] and
reports of strikes in other cities have clearly shaped readers'
strong opposition to strikes in the schools.

As usual in GH polls, one thousand members of the Consumer Panel were asked which of two opposing statements
by experts on the controversial issue they support. The vote
was 74.6 per cent in agreement with former New York State
Senator William F. Condon, cosponsor of New York's Condon-Wadlin law which prohibits strikes by public employees.
Only 22.9 per cent agreed with Mrs. Elizabeth D. Koontz,
who was president of the National Education Association at
the time she wrote her statement for the GH poll. She is now
serving the Nixon administration as director of the Women's
Bureau of the Department of Labor.

Against Teachers' Strikes

Most of the readers who would forbid strikes echo ex-
Senator Condon's view that since teachers always have advance knowledge of salaries, promotions and working conditions any strike action on their part becomes an act of bad
faith. Readers on the whole tend to label striking teachers as
irresponsible. "Striking demonstrates irresponsibility toward
obligations," says an Ohio mother.

In line with this thinking, many panelists use the word *dedication* in referring to a teacher's attitude toward her work. Some go so far as to state that teachers ought to have a sense of mission. A spirit of dedication, they say, would preclude anything as self-seeking as a strike. From Chicago: "A really good teacher is a dedicated person who enters the teaching profession knowing he will never become a millionaire. If he wants money rather than satisfaction, he shouldn't enter the profession in the first place." From Memphis: "Teachers should have a sense of dedication which is peculiar to their position. A teacher who refuses to teach, but instead walks a picket line is an example I would hate to see put before my children."

Quite a few respondents stress the professionalism of teachers. They tend to think that striking may be all right for truck drivers and longshoremen, but for teachers, doctors and lawyers, it is out of character and in bad taste. A reader from a New York suburb puts it this way: "As professionals, teachers should have higher standards and should not demean their status by striking and walking picket lines. I've personally seen teachers on line shouting, hollering and harassing parents who were against the strike. This whole business of civil servants degrading their standards is a disgrace."

To a few panelists, strikes are equated with rebellion and conjure up distressing images of violence. "Strikes cause tension, pain and bodily injury," says an Illinois mother. A Louisiana reader thinks a strike is comparable to an adult temper tantrum: "If you don't play my way, I won't play."

Also in the antistrike camp are many who put the interests of the children first and foremost. One mother says: "When teachers strike, days and weeks are taken from the learning years of young people—time that is all too short and valuable to be used as a bargaining wedge." Another: "Nothing, absolutely nothing, should keep our children from the classrooms." A West Coast panelist points out that a strike causes a youngster to fall behind in his education and also deprives him of his legal right to schooling. Over and over the phrase appears, "The children are the losers."

For Permitting Strikes

Among readers who side with Mrs. Koontz there appears less tendency to see a strike in terms of selfishness or rebellion and greater readiness to accept it as a sometimes necessary technique of social action. Even so, it is advocated only when all else fails. If grievance channels no longer work, if public officials refuse to right wrongs, if parents fail to support their communities' schools, then what else, these readers ask, is there for teachers to do? A panelist from Colorado makes this strong statement: "Most teachers strike because of bad conditions in schools and lack of real public concern. When taxpayers refuse to recognize the issues, teachers must bring them into focus. If the American public can afford to pay more for entertainment, drinking, smoking and pets than they do for education, something is seriously wrong!"

A New Jersey father, who presumably preempted his wife's questionnaire, says: "Simply because teachers are professionals, their right to strike for fair wages should not be precluded. Indeed, the no-strike clauses in contracts seem to be against fair play. Because teachers have been exploited by the community, the caliber of teachers has seriously deteriorated."

A number of readers point out that a strike may at times serve a useful purpose as a last-ditch effort to arouse a community to its duty. A mother of two preschool children in Holland, Michigan, reports that local teachers' salaries were about the lowest in the state until a strike brought them into line. A former teacher says that sometimes a strike is the only way to "fight city hall." A few panelists make a distinction between strikes called primarily to benefit the staff in terms of wages and those called chiefly to help the students in terms of smaller classes, better curriculum or improved school buildings. They support strikes in the latter category.

One surprising aspect of this poll is the finding that panelists who are now teaching or were formerly engaged in teaching line up with equal vehemence on both sides of the argument. A Missouri teacher with school-age children of her own says: "We teachers are not paid as highly as we should be, but strikes lower our professional image. Strikes are not the answer." A teacher temporarily retired to raise her family admits that she is appalled by the actions of her striking colleagues.

On the other hand, a Louisiana teacher says bluntly: "Most of us teach because we like young people and not for the money. However, our families need food, shoes, dental care just as do those families whose children we teach."

IV. STRIKES: THE UNDERLYING, UNSOLVED PROBLEM

EDITOR'S INTRODUCTION

Can there be viable collective bargaining if the right to strike against the employer is not present? Can strikes by certain categories of government employees be tolerated? What are the acceptable alternatives to the strike?

These are questions which arise uniquely in the area of public sector bargaining. In private industry, many studies have been made and much effort given toward lessening the frequency and impact of strikes, but the strike in itself is generally accepted as "part of the game." Strikes by public employees, at least up to the present, have not been accepted.

The varying attitudes of public employee unions toward strikes is examined in the first selection, and in the second selection Arnold M. Zack, a labor arbitrator, looks to some of the motivations. In the articles which follow, A. H. Raskin of the New York *Times* editorial staff and Jerry Wurf, leader of a public employees' union, take opposite sides on the question of the necessity of prohibiting strikes.

Theodore W. Kheel and Professor George W. Taylor, among the nation's leaders in mediation of public sector labor disputes, urge new approaches to bargaining as strike substitutes. Professor Jack Stieber suggests that strikes in certain classifications of government employment might be acceptable if firm measures can be taken to prevent strikes in other classifications. In the articles that close this section, Representative Benjamin B. Blackburn of Georgia and Henry G. Marsh, former mayor of Saginaw, Michigan, consider compulsory arbitration as a strike alternative.

Several of the articles in this section, especially that by Dr. Taylor, make reference to the fact-finding procedure as a means of avoiding or settling strikes. This procedure, sometimes used in the more critical private sector disputes, involves an investigation by an outside neutral individual or panel. After such study, the "facts" are reported, sometimes with and sometimes without recommendations for settlement. Occasionally, the fact finder becomes involved with the parties and acts as a mediator of the dispute as an adjunct of his investigation. Fact finding in the dispute-settlement procedure is subject to much theoretical discussion today as to its merits and limitations.

UNION ATTITUDES ON STRIKES [1]

An increasing number of unions and employee associations in public service are reexamining the use of strikes to resolve contract disputes. For many years, government employee unions voluntarily included no-strike pledges in their constitutions or operated under longstanding resolutions condemning strikes. However, at their 1968 conventions, two postal unions, the Fire Fighters, and the National Association of Government Employees deleted their no-strike clauses and directed further studies on the strike issue.

These changes in attitude toward the strike occur at the end of a decade during which the number of strikes by public employees has risen steadily. In 1966-67 alone, strikes in the public sector, at the state and local levels, caused more idle man-days and involved more workers than strikes in all the preceding eight years (1958-65).

Federal antistrike laws date from a 1912 prohibition directed at postal employees, who were granted the right to organize but were not allowed to join unions asserting the right to strike. Over the years this bar was extended to cover other Federal employees. In 1947, the Taft-Hartley law [Labor Management Relations Act, Amendments to the Nation-

[1] From "Public Employee Unions and the Right to Strike," by Anne M. Ross, economist, Division of Industrial Relations, Bureau of Labor Statistics, United States Department of Labor. *Monthly Labor Review.* 92:14-18. Mr. '69.

al Labor Relations Act of 1935] reaffirmed this traditional no-strike policy:

> It shall be unlawful for any individual employee of the United States or any agency thereof including wholly owned government corporations to participate in any strike. Any individual employed by the United States or any agency, who strikes, shall be discharged immediately from his employment and shall forfeit his civil service status, if any, and shall not be eligible for reemployment for three years by the United States in any such agency.

Executive Order 10988, issued in January 1962 [see "Executive Order 10988," in Section V, below], formalized the Federal Government's policy toward employee organizations, stating that no employee organization which asserted the right to strike could be recognized. In addition, under the Code of Fair Labor Practices, employee organizations are prohibited from calling or engaging in a strike or any related action. Under Public Law 330 (1955), as amended, individuals are subject to a $1,000 fine and a year and a day in jail for striking, asserting the right to strike, or knowingly belonging to an organization which asserts the right to strike. As a condition of employment, Federal employees must sign an affidavit pledging not to violate the antistrike ban. Since 1946, appropriation bills have included provisions forbidding the payment of salaries to any member of an organization asserting the right to strike against the United States.

Although 29 states grant the right to organize and 16 states order or permit collective bargaining in some form for state or local employees, 35 states, by law and court decisions, prohibit strikes. The Condon-Wadlin Act (1947) in New York State, a model for antistrike legislation during the post-World War II period, provided for reemployment of workers involved in strikes but barred pay increases for three years following the strike. Under the superseding Taylor Law (1967), New York public employees are no longer subject to this financial penalty. However, they can be charged with misconduct, which could lead to dismissal or fines. In addi-

tion, an employee organization can lose its dues checkoff for
up to eighteen months and be fined up to $10,000, or one
week's dues (whichever is less) for each day of the strike, or
at least $1,000. After work stoppages in September 1967 and
January 1968, respectively, both the United Federation of
Teachers and the Uniformed Sanitationmen's Association
lost their dues checkoff and were fined. Union presidents
were jailed for fifteen days and fined $250.

Michigan state employees are subjected to financial penalties and possible dismissal; striking Massachusetts municipal employees are subject to a $100 fine. Other state laws
prohibit strikes but do not specify penalties for violations.
Generally, states granting the right to organize and to bargain prohibit strikes by public employees. No state explicitly
grants public employees the right to strike.

The Issues

Arguments opposing public strikes usually stress the two
following points: First, the government provides essential
services which must not be interrupted; and second, strikes
should not be permitted against a sovereign body.

Government services have traditionally been considered
essential. The classical formulation of this view, perhaps,
was made by Governor Calvin Coolidge during the 1919
Boston police strike: "There is no right to strike against the
public safety by anybody, anywhere, at any time."

Critics point out that all services are not equally essential. For instance, the responsibility of a park attendant cannot be equated with that of a policeman. Others rebut that,
if distinctions are made between more or less essential services, in the long run, no services would be considered essential; all government employees would receive the same
rights (including the strike) as those employees in the private sector.

Supporters of antistrike rules claim that, in theory, neither negotiations with nor strikes against a sovereign body
are possible, since representatives of that government cannot

share authority with employee representatives. President Franklin D. Roosevelt, in a letter to the National Federation of Federal Employees in 1937, outlined the reasons for this view:

> The very nature and purposes of government make it impossible for administration officials to represent fully or to bind the employer in mutual discussions with government employee organizations. The employer is the whole people who speak by laws enacted by their representative in Congress. Accordingly, administration officials and employees alike are governed and guided, and in many cases restricted, by laws which establish policies, procedures, or rules in personnel matters.

Those opposed to stoppages point out that the strike, as an economic weapon, is inapplicable since government will not be put out of business, nor will it use a tactic such as the lockout. . . .

Critics of strike bans claim that collective bargaining has been impeded. William Buck, former President of the International Association of Fire Fighters, asserts that some public managers, knowing that public employees have generally renounced the right to strike, have bargained in bad faith:

> Certain arbitrary public officials, knowing that we cannot and will not strike because we voluntarily gave up the right in 1918 when we were founded, have certainly taken advantage of the professional fire fighters across the board.
> As a matter of fact, the record will show we have been exploited by such arbitrary public officials who ofttime dared us to strike, knowing that we would not.

Without a right to strike, public employee unions claim, there is no lever to pressure public officials to negotiate in good faith. Proponents of the right to strike contend that government employees should have the right to use the same tactics available to workers in private industry, since they have the same interest in improving wages and working conditions.

Advocates of the right to strike, however, do not assert an unqualified right. They argue that the right to strike and

the threat of a strike facilitate collective bargaining and perhaps reduce the number of work stoppages in government.
Jerry Wurf, president of the American Federation of State,
County and Municipal Employees, referred to the strike as
"something to impress the boss." [See "Strike Bans Warp Collective Bargaining," in this section, below.]

The Governor's Commission to Revise the Public Employee Law in Pennsylvania recommended that a limited
right to strike be extended to public employees where work
stoppages do not endanger public welfare, after negotiation
impasse procedures have been exhausted. The Commission
stated:

> The collective bargaining process will be strengthened if
> this qualified right to strike is recognized. It will be some
> curb on the possible intransigence of an employer; and the
> limitations on the right to strike will serve notice on the
> employee that there are limits to the hardship he can im-
> pose. . . . In short, we look upon the limited and carefully
> defined right to strike as a safety valve that will in fact pre-
> vent strikes.

Some union officials agree that collective bargaining must
be improved, but that passing legislation, not deleting no-
strike clauses, will accomplish that end. Absence of no-strike
pledges for Federal unions, they maintain, would only antag-
onize members of Congress who support stronger collective
bargaining legislation for Government employees.

Constitutional Amendments

In 1963, the American Federation of Teachers and, in
1966, the State, County and Municipal Employees issued
policy statements supporting work stoppages in some areas.
In the summer of 1968, four unions dropped their no-strike
clauses and others, mostly Federal, discussed the issue at their
conventions.

Among 20 public employee unions (4 at the state level
and the remainder Federal), 7 have constitutions with explicit no-strike pledges; the constitution of 1 union indirectly
makes this same pledge; and 12 unions have no constitutional

reference to the strike. (See table below.) Included in the latter 12 are the 4 unions which eliminated their no-strike pledges.

Public employee unions and the strike issue, 1968

Union strike policies	Union membership
Strike ban in union constitution:	
Special Delivery Messengers	2,073
National Alliance of Postal and Federal Employees	37,000
Post Office and General Service Maintenance	9,237
Post Office Motor Vehicle Employees	8,141
American Federation of Government Employees	199,823
National Federation of Federal Employees	80,000
ASCS County Office Employees	14,300
Rural Letter Carriers	40,340
Strike ban recently removed from constitution:	
National Association of Government Employees	(See Note)
United Federation of Postal Clerks	143,146
National Postal Union	70,000
International Association of Fire Fighters	115,000
Others having no reference in union constitution:	
Letter Carriers (AFL-CIO)	189,628
American Federation of Teachers	125,000
National Education Association	1,081,660
American Federation of State, County and Municipal Employees	281,277
Postal Supervisors	31,700
Postmasters League	18,000
Postmasters Association	32,717
Post Office Mail Handlers	32,800
Study resolutions and policy statements on strikes:	
National Postal Union	70,000
Letter Carriers	189,628
United Federation of Postal Clerks	143,146
American Federation of Teachers	125,000
National Education Association	1,081,660
American Federation of State, County and Municipal Employees	281,277

NOTE: This table covers only unions which have a majority of their members in public employment. See *Directory of National and International Labor Unions in the United States, 1967.* No membership figures are reported for the National Association of Government Employees. The figures given for the National Education Association are as of May 31, 1968; all others are for 1966.

The National Postal Union, which dropped the no-strike clause, and the Letter Carriers, which had never referred to the strike in its constitution, passed resolutions directing their officers to study the strike issue in Federal employment. Delegates to these conventions were concerned with the Federal employee's right to strike and elimination of the no-strike pledge administered to Federal employees. These two unions and the United Federation of Postal Clerks, which also deleted the no-strike clause, represent about 60 per cent of postal employees.

The National Association of Government Employees was the other Federal employee union which voted without opposition to delete the no-strike clause. On the other hand, the American Federation of Government Employees, after prolonged debate, defeated resolutions to eliminate the no-strike pledge. Similarly, the National Federation of Federal Employees retained its no-strike ban, and President Nathan Wolkomir suggested that the union apply sanctions to agencies guilty of unfair labor practices instead of eliminating the no-strike pledge.

None of these unions, it should be noted, has asserted the right to strike, possibly because they might be penalized under Executive Order 10988 and the Code of Fair Labor Practices, and thus lose their bargaining rights and dues checkoff. The Postal Clerks, for instance, stated: "Under existing restrictions the Federation does not assert the right to strike against the Government." However, it considered the no-strike pledge to be superfluous because of laws prohibiting strikes by public employees.

The four state and municipal unions or associations are among those unions having no reference to strikes. At the 1968 convention, the Delegate Assembly of the National Education Association supported a resolution giving qualified support to affiliates involved in strikes, as had the AFSCME and the AFT. The NEA Board of Directors had approved the policy in 1967, but this resolution was the first official support by the Assembly.

The remaining local employees union, the International Association of Fire Fighters, deleted its no-strike ban before it even considered a fact-finding report, commissioned by the 1966 convention, which retained the no-strike ban but called for modifications in it. The union has no official policy on strikes and no constitutional control over striking locals.

STRIKE MOTIVATIONS [2]

Nearly two million school children throughout the country were denied critical days of education when the fall term began . . . [in 1967] because of disagreements between their teachers and boards of education. Breakdowns in negotiations between the parties over wages, classroom discipline, and managerial responsibility brought a rash of teachers' strikes in New York, Michigan, Illinois, Kentucky, Florida and elsewhere. These strikes, and those of other public employees such as firemen, policemen, transit workers, garbage collectors, and social workers . . . raise serious questions for the public. Are such strikes increasing in number? Why do they occur? Can they be avoided, or hopefully even eliminated?

We have all learned to live with occasional strikes in private industry. Why do we inject a different standard in public employment? Certainly the airline strike in the summer of 1966 caused some disappointment among vacationers and businessmen alike, and the Ford strike of 1967 delayed sporting new auto models to our neighbors. But by and large, these interruptions in industrial service and production are sufficiently irregular and sufficiently remote from our immediate needs, that we have come to accept them as a cost of the free labor market.

Strikes of public employees, however, elicit a different response. . . .

Employees of Federal, state and local governments long protected by civil service rules have belatedly awakened to the fact that workers holding the same jobs in private industry have for a third of a century had the legal protection of the right to form, join and assist labor organizations of their own choosing, to engage in collective bargaining, and to

[2] From "Why Public Employees Strike," by Arnold M. Zack, labor-management arbitrator. *Arbitration Journal.* 23:69-84. '68. Reprinted by permission.

withhold their services if offered conditions of employment that were judged unacceptable. As the services of government move more and more into tasks traditionally performed by privately employed workers, such as provision of light and power, housing, and recreational facilities, there are bound to be more demands for those rights long guaranteed to private industry employees.

This is coupled with the fact that conditions of workers in private industry have surpassed or caught up with those of the public employee. Employees in private industry can win higher pay, shorter hours and better working conditions much more rapidly in an expanding economy, particularly in an era of even mild inflation. Any increased costs are easily passed on to the consumer. Government workers, on the other hand, once wage leaders, tend to be held back in their wage expansion by increasing demands for government services, and protests over rising budgets and tax rates. The existing legislative process of fixing civil service wages is slower, less responsive to direct worker pressures than is collective bargaining. These factors all help to create a wider and wider disparity between levels of compensation for comparable work in private industry and public employment. But, if this difference is not enough to spark public employee unrest, there are also wage disparities within the public employment industry itself.

A few craft unions in public employment, such as building-trades and building-service unions, have been successful through legislation and political pressure in achieving agreement to pay to those in public employment "the prevailing rates" obtainable by their union brethren in private industry. This tends to arouse further the jealousy of other public employees who have lacked the political strength to obtain concessions matching private employment benefits. This disparity may well increase in the future if wages in private industry take an inflationary turn.

This contrast in levels of compensation has led trade unions traditionally active only in private industry, such as the Teamsters Union, the Common Laborers and District Fifty of the United Mine Workers, to begin organizational activities among public employees, particularly as their private industry membership remains constant or shrinks. Public employment is the fastest growing "industry" in the United States, making it an attractive area for the unions to begin organizing. More and more unions are likely to enter this field, thus increasing competition among unions to gain control of this unorganized group.

More Aggressive Organizing and Bargaining

This entrance of unions from the private industry into the public employment industry is spurring several of the unions which have traditionally been involved in organizing public employees, such as the American Federation of Teachers and the American Federation of State, County and Municipal Employees, to adopt far more dynamic programs, and to take far more drastic action when they cannot reach agreement with the employer [see the preceding article]. Even the more traditional National Education Association has begun to invoke sanctions, endeavoring to "outunion the union."

Besides increasing attempts by unions to organize these workers and the differences in compensation between private and public employers, the expansion of government services has attracted into public employment many younger and more highly educated staff people than has been traditional in government service. These new intellectuals come into government service fully aware of the expanded activities of trade unions among professional employees in private industry and far more anxious to gain for themselves and fellow employees comparable improvements in wages, hours and working conditions. Many are short-term employees, but they have their impact on the older, more conservative public employees. They have become active advocates of trade unionism for public employees.

This new-image public employee also appears to be better informed than his predecessors in public employment and brings to his new tasks more knowledge and awareness that public employees in other countries have taken a much more active role in improving their working conditions through militant action. Day-long work stoppages in France and teachers' strikes in Canada and Sweden did not go unnoticed here. [See "The European Experience," in Section VI, below.] Some of these techniques are now being applied to the traditionally unorganized American public employees.

Effect of Executive Order 10988

The state and local public employee need not to look to foreign countries for examples, however. A lively spark among these workers was kindled in 1962 when President Kennedy granted the right of collective bargaining to Federal employees through Executive Order 10988. Although there are still some limitations upon free collective bargaining in Federal employment, and an outright prohibition of the strike, the failure of most local jurisdictions to even match the modest grants of recognition and collective bargaining rights extended by the Federal Government have furthered the unrest among state and municipal employees.

These employees have reacted by striking in a number of situations to obtain even the limited rights of recognition accorded to Federal employees by the Executive Order. For example, in Chicago, employees of the Cook County Department of Public Aid struck in May 1966 in order to get an election for collective bargaining and recognition by the Board of County Commissioners. Public employee problems are intensified by conservative legal rulings such as that by the Attorney General of Ohio that Ohio State University may negotiate with the union of its employees but cannot sign a written contract.

Those few states and municipalities which have given recognition to employee organizations and have negotiated with them on conditions of employment have created a precedent which is being used to support claims by other groups for similar recognition, rights and procedures in other localities.

The impartial Office of Collective Bargaining in New York City, established through agreement between New York City and its employee organizations to resolve disputes involving municipal employees, is indicative of the landmark type program which is likely to be sought by other groups. Several other communities in New York have begun to develop comparable procedures for their own municipal employees. Other states such as Illinois have sought to develop mutually acceptable machinery, as have local governments in Los Angeles and elsewhere.

Even when the movement toward recognition is successful, the labor relations scene may not become peaceful, for even greater problems may be created during negotiations. The limited experience of negotiations in public employment appears to be moving toward larger and larger settlements as the employer seeks agreement "at any cost" to forestall the political disadvantage of having "caused" a public employee strike. Sometimes their efforts are not successful and as more and more employee groups use the strike as a device to exact a little bit more from the employer, the public begins to question the effectiveness of the employer's negotiating team and techniques. It is becoming increasingly noticeable that those representing management lack the experience of the more seasoned employee negotiators. This is particularly true with the liberal "Mr. Clean" type political figure who feels he can handle the union negotiator by placing all his cards on the table in advance, and then pleading public responsibility. More and more this type of politician looks with envy at the techniques of the old school politician and his more effective "back room deals." Unless the public authorities learn to rely on practiced and experienced counsel with private industry experience in their negotiations, they will continue to be "stung" by the realities of collective bargaining negotiations.

But even effective negotiating techniques and the strike ban are not enough to bring labor peace in public employment. There has also evolved in the past few years an increasingly recognizable tendency within our political institutions toward civil disobedience and reluctance to accept laws and traditions as binding and immutable. This is traceable most immediately perhaps to the activities of certain civil rights groups. It has led many protest groups to assert a very vocal role against the establishment and the status quo. Thus the idea of compliance with only "good" laws and decisions of the courts and disavowal and noncompliance with the "bad," has led leaders of various protest groups to abandon their informal and traditional channels of complaint.

This is true not only in political and civil rights areas but also in the area of public employment. There appears to be an increasing refusal to comply with civil service procedures and laws prohibiting the strike of public employees. . . . Despite the bans on strikes these groups continue to exercise their power regardless of legal prohibitions. Their lawlessness is given legislative blessing when amnesties are sought to remove the most powerful groups from the coverage of the law. The most militant law-breaking, injunction-defying groups get better working conditions and their success merely triggers more lawlessness among all other public employee groups.

Finally, regardless of restrictive legislation, adverse court decisions, and any sanctions which might be imposed, public employees have come to realize their ultimate power and are exercising it with little concern for public inconvenience. The issue is resolving itself to one of the power to strike rather than the right to strike. The ineffectiveness of prohibitions and sanctions forces one to conclude that public employees will demand and must receive some form of recognition and collective bargaining rights if work stoppages by public employees are to decrease or be eliminated.

A STRIKE BAN IS ESSENTIAL [3]

What conclusions . . . [can be drawn] on either the correctness or the practicality of trying to sustain the age-old doctrine that there is no right to strike against the government? My own conviction is that the basic ban, for all the imperfectness of its observance, is essential to orderly government. The reasons were well set forth by the father of the New Deal, Franklin D. Roosevelt, at the very time that he was sponsoring the Wagner Act as a charter of freedom for workers generally. "A strike of public employees," he said, "manifests nothing less than an intent on their part to prevent or obstruct the operations of government until their demands are satisfied. Such action, looking toward the paralysis of government by those who have sworn to support it, is unthinkable and intolerable."

It is true that the multiplication of government services since FDR's day has fuzzed the boundaries between functions that are distinctly the province of government and those that belong in the private domain. Bus lines in one city are publicly owned and their drivers have no legal right to strike; bus lines in a larger city nearby are privately owned and their drivers can strike without making themselves outlaws. Similar contradictions affect many other functions of great importance. Municipal hospitals and voluntary hospitals perform services so indistinguishable that many operate as partners in urban medical centers. Electric utilities are municipally run in some areas and privately run in others. Warships are built in navy yards or in private yards. Some cities do their own garbage collection; others contract the whole thing to private haulers. The overlaps keep growing with the growth in government, and so does the difficulty of explaining to workers why a prohibition on strikes makes

[3] From "The Revolt of the Civil Servants," by A. H. Raskin, former labor correspondent, assistant editor of the editorial page, New York *Times*. *Saturday Review*. 51:27-30+. D. 7, '68. Copyright 1968 Saturday Review, Inc. Reprinted by permission.

sense in a public job when it does not apply at all in an identical job under private operation.

This difficulty has prompted many critics to argue that the only sound criterion for banning strikes should be the essentiality of the service at stake, whether in the public or the private sector. The only trouble with this line of demarcation is that in practice it proves impossible to draw. The experiences in . . . [recent] years of Detroit, Kansas City, and Youngstown, all of which have had strikes of policemen or firemen, reinforce the . . . lesson that any breach in the no-strike principle invites its total destruction. No group, however vital its duties, will submit to quarantine if the rest of the civil service is given a green light to strike.

In truth, it is precisely the unions whose members control the most indispensable services that constitute the real strike problem in the civil service. If clerks in the Registry of Deeds or park gardeners quit their posts in violation of law, the city can sustain their absence for a long period with little sense of crisis. But when the schools close down or the subways stop running or the garbage trucks stay in the garage, the community finds itself helpless in short order. The more essential the service, the greater the chance that the government will have to capitulate.

The real justification for maintaining inviolate the legal ban on public strikes lies in the nature of government as the embodiment of all the people. It is not a business organized for profit; it cannot move away; it cannot lock out its employees. The conventional notion of strikes as tests of strength in which the pressures of the marketplace operate to constrain both management and union simply does not apply. For that reason, a strike against government becomes an interference with the political process, an effort by one segment of the people to misuse its control over a specific service as a weapon with which to bludgeon the entire community into submission.

Such tactics are disturbing enough when they are confined to raids on the public treasury, overreaching any re-

quirement of equity and forcing the diversion of funds needed for education, housing, health, and other underfinanced
civic responsibilities. But strikes in public agencies are increasingly directed toward compelling the community to do
what unions think they ought to do in terms of public policy.
Sometimes, as in . . . [the 1968] New York school strike, the
issues are so fundamental that the viability of the city itself
is placed in doubt. The teachers were not striking for wages
and hours; the underlying element in their walkout was fear
—fear that the demand of Negro and Puerto Rican parents
for a larger voice in running their neighborhood schools
meant vigilantism and a reign of terror against white teachers. The resulting scars will not heal for many years. Indeed,
the spillover of hate has brought a polarization of the black
and white communities that makes vastly more difficult the
solution of all the city's titanic problems. . . .

In many other fields civil service workers are converting
the strike into a political as well as an economic weapon.
When New York announced that it was considering turning
its city-owned hospitals over to their more efficient voluntary
counterparts, it ran up against a union threat to shut down
all the hospitals if the plan went through. Even that pillar
of law and order, the Fraternal Order of Police, has been
reported as weighing a two-day national walkout to dramatize "the need for more public support of law enforcers."
Valid as many of the proposed policy changes may be, questions of this kind should not be resolved under the gun of
a strike. Otherwise, elected officials will become captives of
embattled civil servants, responding to coercion, not persuasion.

Is there a road out of this morass—one that will insure
good wages and decent conditions for public employees, provide a constructive outlet for their ideas on how to make
government better, and also safeguard the people who pay
the bills against the cutoff of essential services whenever the
workers want more than fairness warrants?

Most of the ingredients for a successful insurance policy along all these lines exist in New York's Taylor Law [state legislation] and in the parallel procedures of Mayor Lindsay's Office of Collective Bargaining. The fact that the city has become a disaster area despite these aids to sane relationships reflects pathetic ineptitude on the city's side of the negotiating table, the deification of power by unions that grew strong without growing responsible, the communication to the union rank and file of the spirit of unreason fostered by their chiefs and, finally, the limited capacity and even more limited will of the citizenry to withstand the privations caused by a strike in a key service.

The antidote, to my mind, does not lie in retrogression to the keep-unions-weak philosophy that goaded the Memphis sanitation workers into striking. No community is entitled to chain its civil servants to their posts on a basis that denies them any collective voice in their conditions of labor or obliges them to subsidize the taxpayers through the acceptance of substandard wages. In the first fourteen months of the Taylor Law, the number of organized state and local employees in New York State rose from 340,000 to 700,000 without a single strike over union recognition. That good accord was finally snapped when the state dawdled overlong in a dispute over a statewide unit for its employees. [See "New York PERB in Action," in Section V, below.] But the basic approach is the civilized way to conduct labor relations in the public sector, and there is no reason why similarly civilized procedures should not prevail in settling disputes over contract terms.

Where direct negotiations and mediation fail, the question of what is fair ought to go to impartial fact finders. But even that is not the end of the line under the Taylor Law. A union that does not like the fact finders' proposals can put its complaint up to the budget-making authorities in the legislature or the city council. That is where the ultimate decision must rest under a democratic system. Making such a system work harmoniously will, of course, depend on the skill, enterprise, and goodwill of the negotiators on both sides.

One thing they will all have to get away from is the "crunch" philosophy that now dominates collective bargaining and that has contributed most to the substitution of muscle for reason in public as well as private labor relations. Equity becomes a refugee when intricate questions of pocketbook or public policy are hammered out in the countdown atmosphere of an impending deadline. The great need in the civil service, even more than in industry generally, is for the development of year-round conference committees in which unions and administrators can exchange ideas and resolve mutual problems. Such committees are particularly well suited to a consideration of the thoughts of those who work in the schools and slums and other trouble spots about what the city could be doing more effectively, more economically, or more humanely in the interests of all its people.

Organized labor has an overall responsibility in this connection: to demonstrate that unionization of the civil service is a force for community benefit and not for community victimization. If the public faces up to its obligation to be a model employer, it has a right to expect all the civil service unions to cooperate in maintaining a stabilized bargaining structure and thus end the whipsaw tactics that made New York's negotiations with its policemen, firemen, and sanitation men so perilous . . . [in 1968]. The unions, in turn, have a right to insist that the no-strike law contain a code of unfair labor practices so that abuses by municipal agencies can be terminated through due process rather than recourse to illegal stoppages.

The worst aspect of the present guerrilla warfare in the civil service is the extent to which contempt for injunctions issued by state courts has become routine in New York and many other communities. Adherence to law cannot flourish when those charged with carrying out the laws exult in flouting them. Sending union leaders to jail is no deterrent; on the contrary, it invests them with a synthetic martyrdom that enhances both their prestige and job security. Fines on the union treasury represent a preferable penalty, provided they are big enough to hurt. But the prohibition on strikes will not survive in the American climate if its maintenance depends primarily on the severity of the penalties for violation.

The test for the country is to prove that, where every reasonable safeguard for just treatment is provided, the rule of law works because it is in the best interest of workers, unions, administrators, and citizens alike to make it work. The lessons New York's teachers taught in the willful misapplication of power have already boomeranged in the adoption by racial extremists of comparable techniques of mass force to terrorize teachers and make a shambles of the initial approaches to community control of schools. The leaders of the police, fire, and sanitation unions in New York have all had bruising experiences with the contagious effects on their membership of the concept that "you get more by being impossible." The community cannot tolerate the notion that it is defenseless at the hands of organized workers to whom it has entrusted responsibility for essential services. But these same workers will be the chief sufferers if their flight from orderly process becomes a guide to action for the rootless and the disaffected and all the others on the outskirts of hope.

That danger will be especially acute if the people in the ghetto identify teachers, policemen, and the rest of the predominantly white workers in the civil service as "the enemy" —the symbol of the hated establishment that has held them submerged in poverty and degradation. New York's brush with chaos in its school strike has demonstrated the immediate danger of such civil upheaval.

STRIKE BANS WARP COLLECTIVE BARGAINING [4]

Collective bargaining is a process that occurs among equals. It is a process to which the American labor movement is committed. It is not always neat, not always orderly, not always precise. It is occasionally disruptive and sometimes inconveniences people.

Nevertheless, we have knowingly, consciously—and wisely—chosen this process in preference to the authoritarianism of price and wage controls and centralized, presumably scientific, administration of our economic activities. With all of its faults, with all of its occasional lapses, with all the exasperation it sometimes induces, it has worked admirably in the private sector. The American Federation of State, County and Municipal Employees, AFL-CIO, is determined that it will have the same opportunity in the public sector.

We live in a country with undreamed of wealth, a staggering productive capacity and the most advanced technology known to man. But, we pay many public employees at levels that would qualify them for welfare supplements. Yet public employee efforts to improve wages and working conditions have been regarded as arrogant and unbridled self-interest and treated in a manner more appropriate to major insurrections.

The disparity, between our affluence and the pay we give public employees, ironically enough operates largely at lower levels and in what we term social services. Executive assistants, administrative heads and top-level staff are recruited and retained by salaries in the $15,000-$30,000 bracket. We appear to have little difficulty in rationalizing this; given market realities and the need for talent, such compensation appears unavoidable. It is at the $4,000-$10,000 level that we balk and resort to pious and passionate declarations of the requirement of a sense of dedication to public service.

[4] From "What Rights Has a Public Employee?" by Jerry Wurf, president, American Federation of State, County and Municipal Employees (AFL-CIO). *Wall Street Journal* 170:18. S. 15, '67. Reprinted by permission.

Denied traditional unionism and collective bargaining, some public employees have historically resorted to lobbying. The postal service is probably the outstanding example. A jungle of administrative regulations and laws for many years prohibited even this. There is a nightmarish quality, in retrospect, to a ruling that provided disciplinary action for a letter carrier who visited Washington on his own time, at his own expense, saw his own congressman and discussed his own working conditions.

Fortunately, this is no longer true.

But even now, a public employee union that turns to legislators to correct inequities is condemned as irresponsible, denounced for flexing political muscle and regarded with the jaundice conventionally reserved for extortion.

It would appear that public employee unionism was inappropriate, collective bargaining illegal and recourse to normal legislative processes immoral.

Perhaps the greatest irony of all involves the evolution of the civil service system. This reform originated in the desire to curb the abuses of patronage and to develop a cadre of competent public servants relatively immune from political vagaries.

It was, at the time, an admirably progressive step, and continues to be a valuable adjunct to the process of running government. The principle of merit employment is not to be discarded lightly.

But the system of civil service ought not be regarded as sacred and immune from the same evaluation and criticism applied to other human instrumentalities. . . .

Recent years have witnessed a sharp increase in government employment and a dramatic spurt in public employee unionism. Some people mutter darkly about the uncontrollable expansion of the Federal bureaucracy. But most of this recent expansion has occurred at the state and local level. Currently approximately 75 per cent of all government is here. The Federal level has been remarkably stable.

We are, therefore, considering one of the fastest growing sectors in our society. Most certainly we are considering the fastest growing sector in the American labor movement.

But the statistics of government employment have a far greater significance. They suggest a major transformation in the structure and nature of our society.

When the Boston police strike occurred in 1919, the private and public sectors were discrete. They were separate entities, relatively easy to distinguish from one another. Even if one adds the necessary qualification that every major form of transportation was heavily subsidized in one form or another, or that government-imposed tariffs provided shelters for our industry, even with all this the world of the private entrepreneur and the world of public enterprise was easily identifiable in 1920.

Things have changed.

In 1920 needy people, if they received any assistance at all, received it from private philanthropies. In 1967, public welfare is a major activity and a significant and growing budget item. Revealingly enough, government involvement has not obliterated private philanthropic efforts; the two complement each other.

Our public school system is staggering under the load of additional students; but private school enrollment climbs correspondingly. State universities are flourishing, but so are their private counterparts, and their roles are indistinguishable. Furthermore, Federal funds underwrite major construction and research programs at leading private universities as well as at public institutions.

The clear demarcation between private and public sectors is gone. With some exceptions, it has vanished beneath a maze of overlapping functions, parallel efforts, incredibly complex relationships.

Magically, all this has occurred without violating our historic apprehension of government. Magically, it has taken place within our democratic framework and, astonishingly, has indeed strengthened it.

If this necessarily brief and admittedly oversimplified summary is valid, then one other thing has occurred: Traditional distinctions between labor-management relations in the private and public sectors have become irrelevant.

One cannot argue logically about the uniqueness of public service confronted by public bus drivers in New York City and private bus drivers in Washington performing identical services.

Reasonable men cannot really be expected to accept the thesis that all public services are equally crucial. The parks attendant is performing an important function, but social catastrophe is not imminent in his temporary absence. That decorative secretary in a government agency is really not performing differently from her sister in the private world.

This assertion has simply been repeated so frequently that it has gained unwarranted stature and credibility.

At the same time, we should not commit a similar error in reverse. Certain public services are undeniably critical, in the same way that some private services are. This federation, consequently, constitutionally regards its police members somewhat differently from its other members.

We argue for reasonable and thoughtful distinctions and against the kind of wholesale, sloppy and unsupportable generalizations with which the public employee sector has been afflicted.

If there is a uniquely American style it is characterized by a pragmatic approach. We have historically tinkered and "made do," preferring the tentative experiment to complex and abstract theorizing.

Discussions of public employee strikes have displayed a regrettable preoccupation with hypothetical constructs and abstract theories (and spurious ones at that). . . . [The AFSCME] constitution recognizes that law enforcement groups cannot be allowed the right to strike. However, the prohibition cannot and must not be applied across the board to all public employees.

We know that public employee strikes have been and are illegal in every jurisdiction that does or does not have a law on the subject.

We know, further, that in some jurisdictions the penalties for violation of the strike prohibition are relatively mild and in others they are extremely harsh.

We know, in addition, that in some places elaborate labor-management machinery has been devised and in others no structure is visible.

We also know that public employee strikes have occurred in jurisdictions that proscribed them.

They have occurred where the penalties were mild and where the penalties were severe.

They have occurred where there was special legislation and elaborate machinery and in the absence of both legislation and machinery.

Court injunctions and confiscatory fines have not been demonstrably successful in the private sector; limited experience suggests they will be no more successful in the public sector.

Strike prohibitions are not simply ineffectual, though they are undeniably that. What is far more serious, they warp the vital process of collective bargaining. They bring employees to the bargaining table, but as inferiors. Simultaneously, they provide false reassurance to management representatives and induce less-than-genuine negotiations. Ironically, they create the very tensions, exacerbate the very situations, provoke the very strikes they were allegedly formulated to prevent.

It is time we learned from experience. Until quite recently, management and workers in the public sector appeared trapped in a grotesque minuet, the score for which was written a half century ago.

The democracy of our political life deserves full extension into the labor relations of our public life. Public employees will not have it otherwise.

IMPROVE THE BARGAINING PROCESS [5]

I believe we may be able to devise a law of public employment relations that is workable, one that will avoid strikes that injure the public interest while affording equitable treatment to public employees. By taking this course we can develop techniques that are responsive to the complex changing conditions and personalities of labor relations. Such a program should, I suggest, follow these broad lines:

First, it should distinguish between terms of employment set directly by the legislature and those which by delegation or established practice fall into the area defined by the Taylor Committee [to revise New York State public employee legislation] as suitable for collective negotiations. The law can affirm the principle that there can be no collective bargaining with the state legislature. It is not equipped to bargain over the terms of legislation with any one group. Its status as the lawmaker for all the people must be preserved and its process should be invoked only by political appeal, not by the pressure of withheld services. Since there cannot possibly be real bargaining on those terms and conditions of employment determined directly by the state legislature, there can be no lawful strike in such situations. This is presently the case for certain classifications of civil service employees, including stenographers and clerks, hospital attendants and correctional officers, where it is believed that statewide wage uniformity is desirable. But wherever authority can feasibly be delegated, an agent should be designated with whom the employees can bargain over those terms and conditions included in the delegation.

The Taylor Committee said that the "legislative body of the government involved" must have the final word and they seemed to suggest that these lawmakers should be ready

[5] From "How to Prevent Strikes by Public Employees," by Theodore W. Kheel, lawyer and noted labor-management mediator. In *Proceedings of New York University Twenty-first Annual Conference on Labor* [conducted by the New York University Institute of Labor Relations, May 13-16, 1968]; ed. by Thomas G. S. Christensen. Bender. New York. '69. p 566-75. Copyright © 1969 by New York University. Reprinted by permission.

to consider the merits of individual disputes if all the other procedures failed. The Committee said that they should hold a show-cause hearing. Although this was omitted from the law [as passed by the New York State legislature] the implication that a legislative body might concern itself with the details of a settlement remains. If this includes the state legislature, I think it is a mistake. When recourse to the state legislature is taken, it should deal solely with the manner of settlement and not the merits of the issues in dispute.

In this respect the state legislature can be distinguished from law-making agencies in political subdivisions of a state. Under the Federal Constitution the states are recognized as sovereign units with appropriate powers. Those powers must be accommodated to the Federal interest but within those bounds the state has primary and residual power. Ultimately, the power to delegate authority and the power to raise revenue and apportion resources among programs of public benefit rests with the state and the state officials. This in no way derogates the importance of home rule or the critical necessity of permitting local governments to devise those measures appropriate to meet their particular problems. . . .

Second, where the legislature has designated an agency with authority to negotiate with the employees, we should pursue a course of encouraging collective bargaining to the fullest extent possible consistent with the public interest. By taking this approach we preserve the flexibility necessary in an area so touched with human factors. We also concentrate on creating an atmosphere more congenial to effective settlement and in this way we better ensure that legal prohibitions and court orders will be obeyed when they are issued or applied. This approach requires that we acknowledge that collective bargaining depends on the prospect of the strike; that we then concentrate on improving the practices of bargaining and the skill of all the participants rather than engrafting misleading and cumbersome procedures onto the machinery. . . .

Third, where collective bargaining fails to yield agreement and an impasse is reached, obviously the law must provide machinery for protecting the community against strikes that imperil the health or safety of the people. But resort to this machinery need seldom be required especially if we seek affirmatively to improve the practice of collective bargaining. In such isolated cases, however, the public interest can be protected, I submit, by techniques for resolving impasses similar to those in Taft-Hartley for the resolution of emergency disputes. This would provide for the issuance of an injunction for a limited period of time, eighty days in the case of Taft-Hartley, during which further efforts to settle the dispute can be made.

Finally, where all these procedures fail to resolve the dispute, the legislature should be prepared to act as the Federal Government has twice acted in national railroad disputes when a legal strike occurred. But the legislature should not be a participant in negotiations. Its proper role is to consider the best steps to resolve the dispute including the possibility of referring the matter to binding arbitration as a last resort. [See "Compulsory Arbitration: Inescapable" and "Compulsory Arbitration: A Pandora's Box," in this section, below.] It then has the responsibility of framing the specific issue or issues that will be submitted to third-party determination. At every stage of the dispute the parties should be encouraged to resolve the dispute themselves by agreement or by referring all or some of the issues voluntarily to arbitration. . . .

I suggest, then, that there is no workable substitute for collective bargaining even in government and that in improving the practice of bargaining lies our best chance to prevent strikes against the public interest. . . . [Recent] experience . . . should demonstrate to us with dramatic clarity that strikes are not prevented by laws emphasizing complex procedures and penalties. The key to preventing strikes in the public no less than the private sector will be found only through improving the bargaining process, not by replacing it. For this purpose we should devote our energy not toward devising new penalties and more intricate procedures but toward improving the understanding and skill of bargaining participants. In the end labor relations must depend on the human factor. The most elaborate machinery is no better than the people who run it. It cannot function automatically. With skillful and responsible negotiators no machinery, no outsiders and no fixed rules are needed to settle disputes.

STRIKE SUBSTITUTES [6]

A strike prohibition in public employment should be effective if ways and means other than the strike are available to insure a fair and equitable disposition of employee claims. We know from experience that finding a substitute for the strike is the formula successfully followed in other situations in which the work stoppage method of settling differences gave unsatisfactory results.

Ironically enough, it was the unions, especially in the mass production industries, which, many years ago became disenamored of the strike as a means of resolving their differences with employers over whether there would be collective bargaining. The election under government auspices was substituted for the organizational strike. This was done over the angry opposition of employers who, more often than not, had been able to withstand the strike pressures.

Then came the substitution of grievance arbitration for strikes during the term of the labor agreement. This was done by labor-management agreements. The development of grievance arbitration was gradual and its widespread adoption was dependent upon overcoming the deep-seated skepticism of both union and management officials. Now, we have to grapple with the problem of creating substitutes

[6] From "Strikes in Public Employment," by George W. Taylor, Harnwell Professor of Industry, University of Pennsylvania, labor-management arbitrator and mediator, and chairman of the commission whose recommendations were acted upon in New York State's Taylor Law. *Good Government.* 85:9-15. Spring '68. Reprinted by permission.

for the strike in public employment. It is not as unique a problem as some folks seem to think.

In testimony before the Presidential Review Committee on Labor-Management Relations in the Federal Service, AFL-CIO President George Meany made some cogent remarks about this problem. He stated: "We believe that it is essential to devise an impartial and orderly procedure to settle unresolved disputes in the Federal service which can be an effective substitute for the right to strike. Otherwise, the right to organize and bargain collectively loses substance and becomes an empty force." He then called for the establishment of a Federal Disputes Panel to mediate and to "assist the parties to arrive at a settlement through other voluntary methods the Panel considers appropriate" or to "hold hearings and make a final, binding decision on the matters in dispute."

The proposal, Mr. Meany emphasized, was made in response to the peculiar problems facing unions that must deal with the Federal Government and "should not be construed as indicating any lessening of our opposition to compulsory arbitration of labor-management disputes." The proposal, he stated, "calls for voluntary acceptance of permanent arbitration machinery by both parties." I take this as an emphasis upon the responsibility of the parties to a particular negotiation to work out mutually acceptable substitutes for the strike.

In general, this phrasing of the problem of dealing with the impasse in government-employee negotiations was much like that which the Governor's commission in New York enunciated. [The commission was chaired by Professor George W. Taylor. See "New York's Taylor Law," in Section V, below, for a fuller discussion of the legislation.—Ed.] There is still the question of what to do if the parties do not agree upon a substitute for the strike. For reasons expressed hereafter, the commission recommended that a binding and final determination should then be made by the legislative bodies rather than by an "outside board" or by an administrative agency of the government.

The commission's concern, however, was not limited to employees of the state of New York. It extended to the employees of the vast number of subordinate political jurisdictions of the state which have varying degrees of sovereignty and widely diverse existing management-labor relationships. Most public employees in New York are not employed by the state, but by its more than 5,500 political subdivisions. They include 62 counties, 932 towns, 533 villages, 62 cities, and nearly 1,200 school districts. It seemed to us that latitude should be given to the representatives of particular functional or occupational groups of employees to work out with the local governmental agencies the mutually acceptable substitute for the strike which seemed to them to be best adapted to their particular circumstances. Numerous alternatives for the strike have been spelled out in the committee report.

Only if the negotiators in the subordinate jurisdictions are unable or unwilling to negotiate do strike substitute procedures established in the state law become applicable to them. The extent to which the state law has to be invoked in local jurisdictions, then, depends upon the willingness of unions, and of administrative agencies as well, to recognize that governmental labor-management relationships are "different."

A vital subject matter of their negotiations is voluntary agreement upon effective substitutes for the strike. Article 209, Section 2 of the state law deals with this matter as follows:

Public employers are hereby empowered to enter into written agreements with recognized or certified employee organizations setting forth procedures to be invoked in the event of disputes which reach an impasse in the course of collective negotiations. In the absence or upon the failure of such procedures, public employers and employee organizations may request the board (i.e., the state public employment relations board) to render assistance....

In my judgment, this section is one of the most important
in the entire law. An opportunity is provided for those who
work directly together in the public service in subordinate
jurisdictions to create their own relationship to insure the
maintenance of law and order.

The procedures outlined in the so-called Taylor Law
which constitute a substitute for the strike, then, apply to
state employees and in those subordinate jurisdictions where
the union and the agency have not agreed upon their own
procedures. Of course, extensive mediation is provided for.
Only upon the failure of negotiation and mediation is there
to be a resort to that provision of the state law under which
a fact-finding board shall "transmit its findings of fact and
recommendations for resolution of the dispute to the chief
executive officer of the government involved and to the employee organization involved, and shall simultaneously make
public such findings and recommendations. . . ."

This is a controversial provision. Many of us who have
had extensive mediation experience in the private sector
have learned that there are times when recommendations of
"fact finders" can either assist or impede agreement. Those
who oppose mandatory recommendations in public service
misread this experience in the private sector because this is
where the right to strike exists as the ultimate determinant.
They are unwilling to face up to the realities of public employee relations, and would accept the possibility of an illegal strike as a vital force in inducing agreement. . . . This is
not appropriate in the public sector. Where the right to
strike is incompatible with the public interest, recommendations must be viewed in a different light. Even as respects
the private sector, one of the most criticized terms of the
emergency disputes provisions of the Taft-Hartley Act is its
withholding from the Boards of Inquiry the power to make
recommendations. . . .

The Governor's committee carefully considered, and, in
its recommendations rejected, the proposal for giving the

fact-finding board a power to make final and binding decisions. The reasons were stated as

not merely because there may be serious questions as to its legality but because of the conviction that impasse disputes may arise less frequently and be settled more equitably by the procedures outlined in this report. In our judgment, the requirement for binding arbitration would likely reduce the prospects of settlement at earlier stages closer to the problems, the employees and the agency; it would tend to . . . encourage arbitrary and extreme positions on both sides. . . .

It follows that, under the New York law, either a governmental agency or an employee organization may reject the recommendations of a fact-finding board. However, rejection by the agency does not constitute a final disposition of the dispute. Nor does rejection by the union make a strike legitimate or appropriate. In public employment, responsibility for final resolution of the dispute lies with the local or state legislative body. These bodies are responsible to the public at large. They must provide the funds or enact any required legislation. The recommendations of a fact-finding board accompanied by the comments on them by the agency and by the union should facilitate the necessary actions of the legislative body. Rather than an arbitration board of "outsiders," it is ultimately the legislature and the political process which have to balance the interests of public employees with the rest of the community. They must, as well, relate the compensation of public employees to the tax rate, and appraise the extent and quality of public services and the efficiency of their performance and relate this to the aspirations of public employees. The recommendations of an impartial board should provide the legislature with a better basis for carrying out its responsibilities than if it started off with only the extreme, and perhaps self-serving, allegations of the disputants.

In contrast to the Condon-Wadlin Act [which it superseded], the so-called Taylor Law embodies an altogether different approach toward the penalties which can be enforced for illegal strikes. In addition to the penalties for contempt of court, i.e., for violation of an injunction, there is a possibility of revocation of checkoff for eighteen months. This particular penalty can be imposed only after a hearing conducted by the Public Employee Relations Board. At the hearing the board must consider: (1) whether the employee organization called the strike or tried to prevent it; (2) whether the employee organization made or was making good faith efforts to terminate the strike; and (3) whether, if so alleged by the employee organization, the public employer or its representatives engaged in such acts of extreme provocation as to detract from the responsibility of the employee organizations for the strike.

In the final analysis, however, the question of whether strikes of public employees can be minimized or eliminated depends not primarily upon those penalties. Rather, the answer depends upon the willingness and ability of union organizations and public employers to accept the challenge and the responsibility for working out their own relationships. This includes the perfection of negotiating procedures and the creation of substitutes for the strike. Unions have to recognize the inappropriateness of strikes. The governmental agencies have to believe in the right of employees to participate effectively through representatives of their own choosing in the establishment and administration of their employment terms. This is not an easy answer but it is, I believe, a realistic one.

WHEN STRIKES MAY BE PERMITTED [7]

The United States has come a long way in dealing with public employee-management relations during the last few years. Future progress will depend, in part, upon how we

[7] From "A New Approach to Strikes in Public Employment," by Jack Stieber, director, School of Labor and Industrial Relations, and professor, Department of Economics, Graduate School of Business Administration, Michigan State University. *MSU (Michigan State University) Business Topics.* 15:67-71. Autumn '67. Reprinted by permission of the publisher, the Bureau of Business and Economic Research, Division of Research, Graduate School of Business Administration, Michigan State University.

handle the difficult problem of public employee strikes. What are the lessons of past experience for future policy on this issue?

1. The right to join employee organizations and to negotiate with their employers through representatives of their own choosing should be guaranteed to all public employees at all levels of government, by Federal legislation, if necessary. Government employees in backward states should not be denied these fundamental rights.

2. Governments have a responsibility to promote settlements without interruption of public services. This includes provision for mediation and fact finding with recommendations in all disputes in which an impasse has been reached in negotiations.

3. Employee organizations and public employers in all government services should be encouraged to develop their own procedures to resolve disputes without interruption of work (including the use of voluntary arbitration). Long experience in private industry has demonstrated that the parties are usually better satisfied with their own solutions than with those imposed from the outside.

4. Regardless of preventive measures or prohibitions and penalties provided by law, strikes in government will occur. Government policy toward such stoppages should take into account the nature of the service provided and the impact upon the public. There is no more reason to treat all strikes in government alike than there is to apply the same yardstick to all stoppages in private industry. Just as a work stoppage on the railroads or waterfront is handled differently from a strike in a widget factory, so should a strike of policemen or fire fighters be regarded differently from an interruption of service in state liquor stores.

5. Public services should be classified into three categories: those which cannot be given up for even the shortest period of time, those which can be interrupted for a limited

period but not indefinitely, and those services in which work stoppages can be sustained for extended periods without serious effects on the community.

With respect to the first category, which in my opinion would include only police and fire protection and prisons, compulsory arbitration should be used to resolve negotiation impasses but only after all other methods have failed. [See "Compulsory Arbitration: Inescapable" and "Compulsory Arbitration: A Pandora's Box," in this section, below.]

Strikes in the second group of services, which would include hospitals, public utilities, sanitation and schools, should not be prohibited but should be made subject to injunctive relief through the courts when they begin to threaten the health, safety or welfare of the community. The courts, in deciding whether or not to issue injunctions, should consider the total equities in the particular case and should utilize their traditional right to adopt sanctions against those violating injunctions to the particular situation, as recommended in the report of the [Michigan] Advisory Committee on Public Employee Relations. . . . The term *total equities* includes not only the impact of a strike on the public but also the extent to which employee organizations and public employers have met their statutory obligations.

Work stoppages in government activities which do not fall into either of the above classifications should be permitted on the same basis as in private industry.

These changes in public policy will come slowly, if at all. Experimentation with different approaches in the states is desirable and should be encouraged. Eventually, however, I believe that laws dealing with employee-management relations in government will tend toward greater uniformity because the nature of public employment differs little among states, and employee organizations, which are national in scope, will insist on equality of treatment for all government employees.

COMPULSORY ARBITRATION: INESCAPABLE [8]

I generally oppose compulsory arbitration. . . . However, I think we all recognize that Government employees are in a unique position and, because of the uniqueness of their position, compulsory arbitration between Federal employees and agency heads is inescapable. The right to strike and the economic pressures upon employer and employee alike, which are created by strikes in the private sector, would not be present in disputes and resulting strikes in the Federal establishment. In fact, should a strike occur in the Government establishment, as we have witnessed . . . [recently], for example, the garbage strike in New York and teachers' strikes in several states, what is adversely affected is the public good and not the profits of a private business establishment. I think we would all agree that the welfare of the public is too valuable a right to be seriously damaged or hindered where the dispute involves public employees. Thus, I accept and support compulsory arbitration as a final means of settling such disputes.

I do confess, however, that I am not in sympathy with the machinery proposed in . . . legislation [before Congress in 1968]. I do not think that the proposal of having all the arbiters appointed by the President is fair to the employees. . . . If arbitration is to work in practice, as well as theory, it must have the uninhibited sympathy of the employees whose careers are directly affected. It would be my suggestion that the agency head himself should have authority to select two arbiters. He should be free to select these arbiters from any sector of our society. In like measure, I would suggest that the head of the union or the chief spokesman for the aggrieved employees should have equal freedom in selecting two arbiters to represent his position.

[8] From statement by Representative Benjamin B. Blackburn (Republican, Georgia), July 11, 1968. In *Employee-Management Relations in the Federal Service;* hearings before the Committee on Post Office and Civil Service on S. 341, July 11-12, 1968. United States. Congress. Senate. 90th Congress, 2d session. The Committee. Washington, D.C. '68. p 23-7.

The final selection would be three arbiters who would themselves be selected by the four arbiters previously selected. I would suggest that these three arbiters be selected by the vote of a majority of the four previously selected arbiters. These three arbiters should be chosen with a view toward strict impartiality. I should think that these three arbiters should not be presently employed by, either in a managerial capacity or otherwise, any Federal agency. Former employees or department heads might be acceptable, provided that they had not been so engaged for a period of no less than eighteen months.

I sincerely believe that an arbitration board of seven members selected as I have outlined above could resolve differences in an impartial manner. More importantly, such an arbitration board could enjoy the confidence of the employee, the agency, and the general public, and further could protect the legitimate interests of each.

COMPULSORY ARBITRATION: A PANDORA'S BOX [9]

The [Michigan] legislature has repeatedly considered legislation which would provide for binding, compulsory arbitration of disputes between municipalities and fire and police. . . .

The Michigan Municipal League has consistently opposed this type legislation for the following reasons, among others. One of the basic tenets of local government is that the local elective official has the responsibility to make decisions involving his community, and that he is, at the polls certainly, accountable for those decisions. Responsibility and accountability are inseparable.

His responsibilities cover broad and often overlapping, almost invariably competing interests—services, capital expenditures, general welfare, employees, to name only a few. He shares with officials at all levels of government, an abun-

⁹ From article by Henry G. Marsh, attorney, former mayor, Saginaw, Michigan, and chairman, Michigan Municipal League Employee Relations Committee. *Michigan Municipal Review.* 41:227+. S. '68. Reprinted by permission.

dance of legitimate, competing demands and a scarcity of money. His success in leading his community depends in great degree on the exercise of his best skill, judgment and perceptiveness in balancing, weighing and accommodating competing needs and desires. His response as an elected official must be conditioned by his very real awareness of his accountability to the electorate for his stewardship. Responsibility demands accountability.

All efforts which I have seen so far to provide for compulsory arbitration of public employer-employee disputes seem to place responsibility for making decisions in the hands of people who have little or no familiarity with the staggering perplexity and frustration involved in meeting local needs but at the same time leave the accountability for success or failure to the elected official.

A typical arbitration panel would consist of three members—one chosen by the public agency, one by the union and the third member chosen by the other two. Assuming, and I think with some reason, that the first two tend to identify with the appointing authority, the third member is in fact the decision maker. He, or all three, may be totally unacquainted with the community, its needs and its goals.

Let me hasten to say that I am not implying that nowhere in this state can three people be found who will honestly and earnestly listen to the facts and arguments and make a fair decision. I am saying that the scope of the decision which they are called upon to make is in no sense comparable to that which the public official faces. They must determine (1) whether the employee demands are reasonable; and (2) whether the city has money to pay out its available funds. Presto, the decision is made.

Yet, . . . this is only the beginning when budget time rolls around: What about streets and pavement, sewers, recreation, civic centers, urban renewal, services—and other employee groups—all competing, all legitimate and all with vociferous proponents. Unless arbitrators are fully cognizant of the full range of needs, demands and choices, as well as the political ramifications involved, they cannot possibly make informed judgments for the overall good of the *entire* community. In effect, they would usurp . . . [the elected officials'] role by determining . . . priorities without even being aware of the alternatives. This strikes me as being a clear and present danger to the very concept of home rule.

A few years ago, the Michigan legislature considered a compulsory arbitration bill which attempted to lay down guidelines for the arbitrators. It provided, among other things, that in determining whether a wage increase was justified, the taxing ability of the municipality could be considered. In Saginaw, we have a ten-mill property tax limitation but we levy six mills. Obviously, we can raise taxes by approximately 40 per cent, so why do we not have adequate money for substantial raises? Well, the reason is that we have an income tax and we pledged a cut in the property tax of four mills to our citizens to get the income tax approved and because we felt this more equitable. We have respected that pledge despite the fact that there is no legal impediment to raising taxes. Would an arbitrator who had no part in that decision feel bound by that pledge in the face of insistent and perhaps justifiable demands from employees? You be the judge.

I cite the experience of Saginaw with the International Association of Fire Fighters as a classic example. This occurred, incidentally without benefit of a law, just because they thought it would pass.

The following is extracted from notes of the Saginaw Management Negotiating Team for 1968:

May 9. Initiated meeting with IAFF. Requested $2500 increase across the board or 35 per cent increase. Requested immediate counteroffer from the city. The city requested a more detailed breakdown of the union demand, particularly with regard to fringe benefits. The union refused.

May 21. The city made a counteroffer of 5 per cent or $400 across the board at the option of the union. There was an immediate rejection and an indication that a mediator would be requested.

June 10. This was the first meeting with the mediator. A union official is reported as saying "Bill 3725 (Compulsory Arbitration) is going to solve our problems and put an end to all this." Still no additional demands were made.

Later that day, the mediator said that he didn't feel much bargaining could be done today. They were interested in fact finding. He said that he had explained to the union representatives that for an issue to be considered in fact finding, it must first be considered in mediation and further suggested that they be prepared to bargain at the next session.

June 12. The union presented a list of sixteen demands in addition to the original $2500 demand, upping the cost an estimated 50 per cent to 70 per cent from the May 9 figure. Incidentally, they had been requested to have their demands in by March 1.

I suggest that you compare the above sequence of events with the statement by Rev. Fr. Charles Quick of the Economics Department of Providence University, Rhode Island, when he spoke in favor of compulsory arbitration (which was enacted, incidentally) : "Arbitration of any form is resorted to only when negotiations reach an impasse. It presupposes negotiations and in fact, its availability encourages both sides to bargain in good faith for a just settlement in the best interests of the community."

Based on not only this discouraging experience but what would seem to be ordinary probabilities, it seems there is no incentive to make a final offer or demand or even a realistic one at the local level. I would doubt seriously that there has been much mediation, much less arbitration, where the intermediaries didn't recommend something between the top offer and the low demand. Hence, it would seem, with this in mind, the employer would offer little or nothing, holding back for arbitration and the employees would demand pie in the sky for the same reason. . . .

It is for these reasons . . . the Michigan League has consistently opposed compulsory arbitration. We realize that there are inequities in the present situation that are terribly frustrating to employees. Yet, the substitution of a remedy which can only lead to chaos is not the answer. We must jointly continue to search for reasonable, useful answers but compulsory arbitration will not and cannot meet the need.

V. THE LAW

EDITOR'S INTRODUCTION

From the layman's viewpoint, the problem begins with the absence of law; that is, the concept of collective bargaining by workers employed by the sovereign government was generally assumed—simply by absence of legal permission—not to exist until recent years. The concept of work stoppages in defiance of government still is without legal support and may never receive it. Most law in the field of public employee bargaining, therefore, is of recent origin and, in most cases, carefully opens the door to representation and collective bargaining but stops short of strike sanction; indeed, specific penalties for work stoppages are an important part of such legislation.

In the first selection Arvid Anderson, head of the New York City Office of Collective Bargaining, examines the overall background for legislative action. Professor Jack Stieber next reviews the impact of President John F. Kennedy's 1962 Executive Order 10988, considered comparable for government employees to the 1935 Wagner Act covering employees in the private sector. This is followed by a draft of recommended changes in Executive Order 10988 which came from a study group named by President Lyndon B. Johnson and probably will receive little consideration by President Nixon's Administration.

State laws in general are reviewed in the next two selections. The final articles in the section deal with New York State's Taylor Law and the Public Employment Relations Board, examining the most recent far-reaching legislation at the state level. Although the law is named for George W. Taylor, who headed several study commissions for the legislature, it should be noted that Professor Taylor repeatedly points out that the law as adopted and later amended in-

cludes numerous provisions devised by the New York State
Legislature not in consonance with his group's recommendations.

THE NEED FOR LEGISLATIVE ACTION [1]

Two strikes by garbagemen have had the most [recent]
significant impact on public collective bargaining. . . . The
New York [City] sanitation strike escalated from a labor dispute to a health emergency to a political crisis which was
ultimately settled by binding arbitration. A strike by garbage collectors in Memphis, Tennessee, for union recognition, provided the scene of a tragedy, the consequences of
which America has only partially comprehended. Both of
these strikes have had and will continue to have long-range
political, economic, and social impact far beyond the immediate interests of the parties involved.

The Memphis strike demonstrated the relationship between collective bargaining and the civil rights struggle and
showed that collective bargaining can be a means for economic and social improvement of minority groups. The
New York sanitation strike pointed the way towards a new
approach in solving contract negotiation disputes in the public sector. One of the lessons which the nation can learn
from the Memphis tragedy is the imperative need for state
and local governments to establish orderly procedures for
collective bargaining in public employment. Today the various states and municipalities need a Taft-Hartley Law [La-
bor-Management Relations Act of 1947] for public employees, a law that provides union recognition, with appropriate
limitations on the right to strike.

    [1] From "Public Employees and Collective Bargaining: Comparative and
Local Experience," by Arvid Anderson, chairman, Office of Collective Bargaining, New York City. In *Proceedings of New York University Twenty-first
Annual Conference on Labor* [conducted by the New York University Institute
of Labor Relations, May 13-16, 1968]; ed. by Thomas G. S. Christensen. Bender.
New York. '69. p 451-69. Copyright © 1969 by New York University. Reprinted
by permission.

A comprehensive collective bargaining statute in public employment would guarantee employees and employers the same rights and protection that their counterparts have in the private sector with appropriate limitations on the right to strike. There would be the right to organize and bargain collectively over wages, hours, and working conditions. There would be rules of fair conduct and protection against unfair labor practices by employers and employee organizations. Administrative machinery would be established for the purpose of determining questions of representation including appropriate bargaining units and for the enforcement of the rights granted by the statute. The statute would provide machinery to resolve disputes which arise during the term of the collective bargaining agreement by mediation and grievance arbitration. Lastly, the statute should provide for the resolution of disputes over the terms of the new labor agreement including disputes over the subject matter of bargaining. The impasse machinery would include advisory arbitration or fact finding with recommendations, and authorize the parties to enter into voluntary and binding arbitration.

Unfortunately, the Memphis lesson, of the need for orderly collective bargaining laws, has not yet been learned, at least not in that city. The City of Memphis, which signed an agreement with sanitation men on the casket of Dr. Martin Luther King [assassinated while in Memphis to rally the strikers], . . . refuses to recognize or bargain with representatives of its police and fire services. . . .

But Memphis is not alone. It is only a symbol. The right to organize and bargain collectively in public employment is not an accepted fact in a majority of the states. While constructive and progressive laws have been established and administered in New York, Connecticut, Massachusetts, Rhode Island, Wisconsin, Minnesota, Michigan, Oregon, and other states, the majority of states have taken no action or at best halting steps to implement the collective bargaining process. To those who believe that collective bargaining laws provoke public employee strikes and discord, look at the record in the states where no collective bargaining laws exist. Recent events in Ohio, Illinois, Florida, Georgia, California, Kansas, and others would demonstrate that strikes in public employment will occur in states that have no collective bargaining laws, as well as in those that have them. The real question is whether there will be orderly procedures to deal with the causes of public employee unrest.

The hour for state action is late. It is my view that the states must act soon or the Federal Government ultimately will. . . .

If a Federal law should be enacted, it is likely to take the pattern of the Equal Opportunities Commission legislation which provided that, unless states enact laws equal or superior in coverage to the Federal law, the Federal law will prevail. There have already been some calls in public employee union circles for such legislation, but a division among the unions as to whether Federal legislation would impede the right to strike has so far discouraged some unions from pressing for Federal legislation at this time.

I believe that the federalization of state and local employment relations would be unfortunate as a confession of failure on the part of the states to regulate the labor relations of their own employees. I do not wish to suggest, however, that the competence and expertise of the Federal Mediation and Conciliation Service [which deals with private sector disputes and to a limited degree with disputes involving Federal agencies] and the National Labor Relations Board [which presently deals only with labor relations in the private sector are] not adequate to deal with the majority of public employee-employer disputes. Again I submit that the vacuum that exists in state and local employment relations will not continue to exist indefinitely. Congress will be faced with insistent demands for Federal regulation if the states fail to act. The demand for Federal legislation will not be limited solely to public employees, but also to vast numbers of uncovered employees in the private sector employed by hospitals, schools, and in agriculture.

The rapid development of public employee collective bargaining has not waited for the passage of protective laws. Social and economic forces have required lawyers in public employment to recognize the necessity of developing a legal framework to deal with collective bargaining as an existing fact, even if laws expressly authorizing it do not yet exist. The laws of Tennessee do not provide a means of determining questions of representation, but the striking garbage workers [in Memphis] were ultimately recognized.

Recognition strikes are virtually unknown in private employment, but recognition is the second highest cause of public employee strikes. . . . There have been other strikes. The sanitation strike [in New York City] found the public employer and the union agreeing to utilize voluntary and binding arbitration to resolve an emergency dispute. There was no express authority under the state or city statute authorizing this procedure, but it was used without any significant challenge to the city's legal authority to do so.

The Memphis and New York strikes are two of the more dramatic examples of social and economic forces which have caused a rethinking of attorney generals' opinions and court decisions with respect to recognition of public employee unions and arbitration of contract terms. A majority of the conventional opinions hold that unless the public employer is expressly authorized to recognize and bargain collectively with unions, to enter into written agreements or to enter into grievance arbitration agreements, the government cannot do so, or at least cannot be required to do so. Fortunately this legal attitude is changed to deal with the facts of political and economic life. . . .

The Office of Collective Bargaining

An interesting example of the constructive cooperation of a public employer and public employee union is the tripartite agreement which created the Office of Collective Bargaining in New York City. While much of this development is unique to New York City, the concept of consent legislation has been used elsewhere and is applicable elsewhere. The Office of Collective Bargaining is an independent body created by the City of New York pursuant to a written agreement between it and the major unions with which it deals. Its carefully designed tripartite structure provides real assurance of impartiality. Its Board of Collective Bargaining consists of two city representatives, two labor representatives, and three impartial members. The labor representatives are nominated by the Municipal Labor Committee, membership to which is open to all certified public employee organizations. The impartial members are elected by the unanimous vote of the city and labor representatives. The City and Municipal Labor Committee jointly pay the salary and expenses of the impartial members. Mediators, arbitrators, and fact finders must be approved by a majority of the Board of Collective Bargaining before they can be registered. Other examples of tripartite cooperation in dealing with public employment problems are the Connecticut municipal statute, the Wisconsin statute for state employees, the Pennsylvania Study Commission, the Maryland Study Commission, and the Illinois Study Commission. All were the results of tripartite efforts. The tripartite process is no guarantee to success but it does recognize the necessity of involving the public employer, the public unions, and so-called neutrals to deal with the continuing problems of labor relations in the public sector. . . .

Need for Legislative Guidelines

The advent of collective bargaining in public employment has brought a whole host of legal problems which need to be answered. It could be most desirable if legislative guidelines were developed to answer questions as to the right of employees to join labor organizations and the right to refrain from such activity. Other problems which need legislative guidelines are: the right of the majority representative to be the exclusive collective bargaining representative with the right to exclusive dues checkoff; the right of a minority union to present grievances; the duty to bargain collectively on the part of the employer and employee organization over wages, hours, and working conditions and the duty to sign collective bargaining agreements.

Legislative guidelines are also needed to establish procedures for determining whether certain subjects are properly within the scope of bargaining, or within the scope of grievance arbitration procedures. Legislative guidelines would be helpful in determing the relationship of the collective bargaining process to civil service procedures with respect to disciplinary matters, job classifications and promotions. Establishment of legislative guidelines would be helpful also for the resolution of impasses and the fixing of authority to bargain on the part of the public employer. In the absence of legislative or executive guidelines, employee and employer organizations will have to develop their own procedures to deal with public employment collective bargaining, especially in those situations where the unions have enough economic and political muscle to insist that decisions be reached.

Grievance arbitration [of disputes during the term of a labor agreement] has been accepted in a large number of public employee jurisdictions by statute, by court decision, and by contracts as a means of resolving disputes over the interpretation and application of collective bargaining agreements. Consideration of voluntary and binding arbitration as a means of contract settlement has also received increasing attention in public and private employment in the past year. [See "Compulsory Arbitration: Inescapable" and "Compulsory Arbitration: A Pandora's Box" in Section IV, above.] As mentioned earlier, the New York sanitation strike was settled by voluntary and binding arbitration. The Wyoming Supreme Court recently upheld a statute authorizing binding arbitration for disputes over the terms of a new agreement with firemen. A Rhode Island and a Pennsylvania statute now provide for the arbitration of disputes affecting firemen, and the Pennsylvania statute also applies to policemen.

Concerns about unconstitutional delegation of legislative power to arbitrators appear to be answered by the fact that some decisions of an arbitration panel are not self-implementing. Of necessity, those arbitration decisions which require implementation by a legislative body or by executive action must await such final action by the legislature or executive before they can be placed into effect. Thus, if more funds need to be appropriated in order to comply with an arbitration award, the legislature or the executive has the final decision. It would, therefore, seem that the courts might possibly conclude that there are no constitutional prohibitions against the utilization of binding arbitration. Whether such development will enhance the collective bargaining process remains to be seen.

There is a fear, which is somewhat justifiable, that the parties will abandon their efforts to reach solutions by collective bargaining contracts in favor of a settlement by a third party. While this is a sound reason for caution in the use of binding and, particularly, compulsory arbitration, the question arises whether it is a persuasive argument in the face of a strike or threatened strike in an essential public service, such as a police or fire strike.

EXECUTIVE ORDER 10988 [2]

In June 1961 President Kennedy appointed a Task Force, chaired by Secretary of Labor [Arthur J.] Goldberg and made up of high Administration officials, to review and advise him on employee-management relations in the Federal service. Prior to this time the only existing legislation governing re-

    [2] From "Collective Bargaining in the Public Sector," paper presented at the thirtieth American Assembly, October 1966, by Jack Stieber, director, School of Labor and Industrial Relations, and professor, Department of Economics, Graduate School of Business Administration, Michigan State University. In *Challenges to Collective Bargaining;* ed. by Lloyd Ulman. Prentice-Hall. Englewood Cliffs, N.J. '67. p 69-73. © 1967 by The American Assembly, Columbia University. Reprinted by permission of Prentice-Hall, Inc., Englewood Cliffs, N.J.

lations between Federal employees and agencies was the Lloyd-LaFollette Act of 1912, which protected the right of postal employees to join unions and petition Congress. It was, in effect, Congress's response to the "gag order" first imposed by President Theodore Roosevelt in 1902 and made more restrictive by President Taft in 1909. The order prohibited any Federal employee or official from responding to any request for information from any committee or member of Congress "except through and as authorized by the head of his department."

The Task Force report noted that although 33 per cent of all Federal employees belonged to national employee organizations, membership varied greatly among agencies, from the Post Office, in which 84 per cent of employees belonged to unions, to the Department of State where "a careful search uncovered a total of eleven members." There existed within the Executive Branch no policy on employee-management relations. The result was wide variation among agencies in their dealings with employee organizations. In the departments and agencies studied by the Task Force, 22 had no stated labor relations policies; 11 had the "barest minimum of policy" giving employees the right to join or not to join employee organizations; and 21 engaged in discussion with employee organizations on limited local problems. Only the Tennessee Valley Authority [see "Collective Bargaining in TVA" in Section II, above] and the Interior Department had extensive relations with unions and other employee organizations, including mediation and arbitration, and written agreements on pay scales, classifications, hours of work, grievances and fringe benefits.

The Task Force report, submitted in November 1961, served as the basis for Executive Order 10988 which was signed by President Kennedy on January 17, 1962. The Order gave all Federal employees the right to join or not to join organizations of their own choosing, and granted exclusive recognition and the right to enter into agreement with an agency to any organization which represents a majority of the employees in an appropriate unit. In order to attain exclusive recognition, an organization must receive a majority of all votes cast in an election participated in by at least 60 per cent of the employees eligible to vote and present at the installation on election day.

A new feature was introduced by the provision of two lower levels of recognition: formal recognition for organizations with at least 10 per cent of the employees in a unit where no other organization has been granted exclusive recognition; and informal recognition for any organization with less than 10 per cent membership. Formal recognition carries with it the right to be consulted in the formulation and implementation of personnel policies and practices and on matters affecting working conditions. Informal recognition gives an organization the right to be heard on matters of interest to its members.

The Order provided that a dispute over the scope of an appropriate unit be resolved by the Secretary of Labor, who could resort to advisory arbitration. . . .

A Code of Fair Labor Practices, promulgated by the President in May 1963, is roughly equivalent to the unfair labor practices contained in the Taft-Hartley Act, with two important additions: strikes and picketing are prohibited, and employee organizations may not discriminate against any employee with regard to terms and conditions of membership because of race, color, creed or national origin.

Bargainable issues were severely circumscribed by Section 7 of Executive Order 10988 which enumerated "certain matters" reserved for management decision. These include the right to direct employees, to hire, promote, transfer; to assign employees and to suspend, demote, discharge or discipline employees; to relieve employees from duties because of lack of work or for other legitimate reasons; and to determine the methods, means and personnel by which operations are to be conducted. Section 6 (b) of the Order further notes that the obligation to negotiate "shall not be construed to extend to such areas of discretion and policy as the mission

of an agency, its budget, its organization and the assignment
of its personnel, or the technology of performing its work."
These restrictions are in addition to such important conditions of employment as salaries of classified employees, pensions, insurance and other fringe benefits, which are established by Congress.

The strong "management rights" clause which is included
in every agreement goes beyond what is usually found in
agreements in private industry. The kind of subjects included
in agreements negotiated between Federal agencies and employee organizations is illustrated by a 1964 BLS [Bureau of
Labor Statistics] report which listed forty-four types of provisions found in such contracts including: hours of work and
overtime, holiday pay, rest periods, working and/or cleanup
provisions, special clothing, work by supervisors, subcon-
tracting, safety, leave policies, jury duty, craft jurisdiction,
wage surveys, promotions and demotions, reductions in force,
job descriptions and ratings, apprenticeship and training,
checkoff of dues, mediation and advisory arbitration of
grievances. . . .

Union Complaints

Despite the acknowledged success of the Executive Order
in promoting union membership and collective bargaining,
employee organizations would like to see some changes made
in the Order and more particularly in its administration by
individual agencies. Their complaints focus on the following
issues:

1. *Bilateral collective bargaining versus unilateral regulations:* Except for the agency-wide agreements in the Post
   Office and the Railroad Retirement Board, all agreements
   are negotiated at the local level and must be approved by
   the agency head. But personnel managers at the agency
   level have been too restrictive in delegating authority to
   local managers to permit meaningful negotiations. Too
   often they issue rules and regulations on matters that
   should be subject to negotiation.

2. *The grievance procedure:* There are too many exclusions
   from the grievance procedure in most agreements, and
   agencies have rarely been willing to agree to advisory
   arbitration in adverse action proceedings. These include
   position and classification cases, disciplinary cases, and
   disputes as to the interpretation and application of the
   agreement if not based on an individual grievance. In
   some instances management has refused to comply with
   an advisory arbitration award. This has led to demands
   that arbitration be made final and binding.

3. *The scope of collective bargaining:* Despite necessary limitations on matters subject to negotiations, there is far more
   room for bargaining than most agencies permit. Wage and
   salary determination is a good example. While Civil Service determines the content and coverage for grades, an
   agency can permit union participation in developing
   policies for determining grades and steps for its employees.
   But only a few agencies follow this practice. Futhermore,
   for wage board employees, and under the comparability
   principle of the Federal Salary Reform Act of 1962, there
   should be bilateral procedures for selecting comparable
   firms, key jobs and geographical areas to be surveyed for
   determining rates of pay.

4. *Collective bargaining impasses:* Only 10 per cent of all
   agreements provide for outside mediation and 25 per cent
   for fact finding and referral to higher authority in the
   agency when an impasse occurs in collective bargaining.
   Without the strike weapon, these procedures take on added
   importance to a union which is already bargaining from a
   very weak position.

5. *Unfair practice charges:* Hearing officers, selected from
   employees of the agency involved, merely rubber stamp
   the action of supervisors and management officials. A few
   agencies have offered to use outside arbitrators as hearing
   officers, and the Labor Department has encouraged this
   practice. Some unions favor turning over administration

of the Order to an impartial agency or board similar to the NLRB [National Labor Relations Board]. Others would like to see the Department of Labor given more responsibility and the Civil Service Commission less in administering the Executive Order.

Agencies too have had complaints, particularly over the amount of time consumed in collective bargaining and handling of grievances. Their major problem, however, has involved the training of thousands of management officials to carry out their responsibilities under the Order. Unions have also faced this problem with respect to training of representatives and stewards. Both have embarked on extensive training programs, making use of universities which have labor and management education programs.

RECOMMENDED CHANGES IN
EXECUTIVE ORDER 10988 [3]

Executive Order 10988 established a presidential governmentwide policy which acknowledged the legitimate role unions should have in the formulation and implementation of Federal personnel policies and practices. . . . In his memorandum of September 8, 1967, establishing a special Review Committee on Federal Employee-Management Relations, . . . President [Johnson] stated:

The time has come for a public review of our five years of experience under Executive Order 10988—what the program has accomplished and where it is deficient—and for consideration of any adjustments needed now to ensure its continued vitality in the public interest.

The Review Committee finds that a flourishing program exists where before Executive Order 10988 there was only a modicum and, in many cases, even a complete absence of employee-management cooperation in the formulation and

[3] From "Draft Report of the President's Review Committee on Employee-Management Relations in the Federal Service." In United States. Department of Labor. *56th Annual Report, Fiscal Year 1968.* Supt. of Docs. Washington, D.C. 20402. '69. Attachment B. p 1-20.

implementation of the policies that shape the conditions of work for Federal employees. . . . [As of April 1968] 1,238,748 employees are in 1,813 units for which exclusively recognized labor organizations are the bargaining agents. These labor organizations have negotiated 882 agreements. In addition, labor organizations representing Federal employees have obtained 1,172 grants of formal recognition and 1,031 grants of informal recognition. These figures do not reflect the union activity in local Post Offices where there are 24,500 grants of exclusive recognition with 13,058 negotiated agreements and 11,000 grants of formal recognition. It is estimated that over one million Federal employees belong to labor organizations. Under the program established by Executive Order 10988, these labor organizations have gained responsible status, stable and increasing membership, and representation rights that ensure substantial participation by employees in the improvement of personnel policies and practices that affect their well-being.

The benefits from the program have been many. There has been a marked improvement in the communication between agencies and their employees. Employees now actively participate in the determination of the conditions of their work. This participation has contributed significantly to the conduct of public business. The collective bargaining agreements that have been negotiated have given continuity and stability to the labor-management relationship. . . .

During . . . public hearings held in Washington, October 23-27, 1967, the Review Committee was aided significantly by the responsible and mature testimony of the more than fifty agency and labor organization representatives and individuals who appeared before the Committee. In addition, more than fifty others submitted written statements. The statements and written submissions received have provided to the Committee a thorough record from which to work in formulating the recommendations which follow.

Recommendations

A. Central Authority for Program Decision—A Federal Labor Relations Panel

A three-member Federal Labor Relations Panel, consisting of the Secretary of Labor, the chairman of the Civil Service Commission, and the chairman of the Civil Service Commission, and the chairman of the National Labor Relations Board, should be established to oversee the entire Federal service labor relations program, to make definitive interpretations and rulings on any provisions of the Order, to decide major policy issues, to entertain, at its discretion, appeals from decisions on certain disputed matters, to review and assist in the resolution of negotiation impasses, and to report to the President on the state of the program with recommendations. . . .

The Panel should be authorized to oversee the entire Federal service labor relations program; to make definitive interpretations and rulings, as needed, on any provisions of the Order or on major policy issues; to entertain, at its discretion and in accordance with such rules as it may prescribe, appeals from decisions on certain disputed matters; to review and assist in the resolution of negotiation impasses; and, from time to time, to report to the President on the state of the program and make recommendations for its improvement.

The Committee feels that such a Panel would ensure the desired balance of judgment and expertise in the personnel management and labor relations fields. Although armed with full authority, the Panel should use calculated restraint in exercising its responsibilities so as to leave the agencies and labor organizations free to work out their differences to the maximum extent possible without damaging the overall program.

B.   Unit, Representation, Unfair Labor Practice and
     Standards of Conduct Cases

The Assistant Secretary of Labor for Labor-Management Relations should issue decisions in unit,
representation, unfair labor practice and standards of
labor organization cases. Either party should have a
limited right of appeal on major policy issues to the
Panel.

The Committee recommends that the Assistant Secretary
of Labor for Labor-Management Relations be assigned responsibility for the handling of complaints concerning unfair
labor practices on the part of either labor organization or
agency representatives, and for the conduct of representation
elections in addition to his present reponsibility for unit and
representation disputes. The assistant secretary should be
authorized to issue decisions to agencies and labor organizations in all such cases, subject to a limited right of appeal on
major policy issues by either party to the Federal Labor Relations Panel, and to refer cases involving major policy
questions to the Federal Labor Relations Panel for decision
or general ruling. Additionally, he should be authorized to
handle complaints concerning alleged violations of the
standards of conduct for labor organizations.

In the performance of his responsibility, the assistant
secretary should be authorized to request the services and
assistance of employees of the National Labor Relations
Board and of other agencies, as he may deem appropriate.
The necessary costs of such service and assistance should be
paid by the agency involved in the case or complaint.

The assistant secretary should have the authority to require agencies and labor organizations to cease and desist
from conduct violative of the Order, and to require them to
take such affirmative corrective action as he deems appropriate to effectuate the policies of the Order. Enforcement of
decisions of the assistant secretary should be achieved
through (1) publishing and appropriate posting of deci-

sions; (2) the required reporting by the respondent (agency or labor organization), within a specified period, to the assistant secretary of the corrective action taken; and (3) where the assistant secretary finds that necessary action has not been taken, referral of the matter to the Federal Labor Relations Panel for appropriate action. In the event questions arise involving the Department of Labor, the assistant secretary's responsibility should be performed by the general counsel of the National Labor Relations Board.

C. Grievances, Appeals, Interpretation of Agreements

1. The Civil Service Commission should integrate all grievance and appeal procedures in a single system to the extent feasible under existing law.

2. The negotiated grievance procedure and appeals procedure (to the extent permitted by law) should be the exclusive procedures available to employees in the unit.

3. Arbitration should be made available for the resolution of disputes over the interpretation and application of an agreement.

4. Exceptions to arbitrators' decisions should be sustained only on grounds similar to those applied by the courts in private-sector labor-management relations. Procedures for considering exceptions to decisions should be established by the Panel.

The Review Committee is of the opinion based on the testimony presented that, to the extent feasible, all grievance and appeal procedures in the agency should be integrated into a single system, that such a system should permit arbitration, should minimize the number of levels of review, and should prohibit duplicate channels of appeal. Accordingly, it is recommended that as soon as practicable the Civil Service Commission accomplish this objective to the extent feasible under existing law. . . .

D. Procedures to Be Adopted in the Event of Impasses in Negotiations

　　1. The Federal Mediation and Conciliation Service should extend its services to the Federal labor relations program.

　　2. Additional procedures for the resolution of impasses should be made available, including fact finding on the merits of a dispute with recommendations forming the basis for further negotiations, or the arbitration of impasses, or both.

　　3. The parties to an impasse should have the right to request the services of the Federal Labor Relations Panel.

Much of the presentation before the Review Committee pertained to procedures for use if an impasse is reached in negotiations between management officials and organizations granted exclusive recognition.

The Report of the President's 1961 Task Force expressed the concern that in the developing stages of employee-management relations, the availability of arbitration would have the effect of escalating too many impasses to third-party settlement. For this reason, the Task Force opposed the adoption of arbitration during the initial stages of the program and suggested instead that agencies devise other methods of impasse resolution for adoption through negotiation. The Review Committee believes that this concern is still valid.

The Committee feels that ready availability of procedures providing for the final resolution of negotiation impasses could cause the undesired escalation effect whereby the parties, instead of working out their differences by hard, earnest and serious negotiation, continually would take their problems to a third party for settlement. It is generally recognized that agreements voluntarily arrived at through a free collective bargaining system are the hallmark of the industrial democracy enjoyed in this country.

Various devices have been used by departments and agencies during the past six years in helping to bring about settlements in negotiations. They have included joint fact-finding committees, referral to higher authority within the agency and the organization and, to a limited extent, mediation. Each of these has proved its usefulness and should continue to be utilized.

At this stage of the program's development, based on past experience, the Committee believes that Government and organization officials should be free, within law, to negotiate techniques most appropriate to their own needs and circumstances. It feels that departments and agencies, where appropriate, should permit their negotiators to agree to a variety of dispute-resolving techniques.

Toward this end, the Committee recommends that the Federal Mediation and Conciliation Service should extend its services to the Federal labor-management relations program. The Service should, subject to such necessary rules as it may prescribe, provide for the Federal service the same type of mediation assistance that it offers in the private sector without charge to either party. In this connection, parties should be permitted to agree to mediation by persons other than Federal Mediation and Conciliation Service commissioners on a cost-sharing basis. In the area of mediation techniques, the Committee believes that preventive mediation is a useful device that should be utilized, where appropriate, in the Federal service.

Other techniques that should be made available, in addition to those which have already been utilized, are (1) third-party *fact finding* on the merits of a dispute *with recommendations* forming the basis for further negotiations or (2) the arbitration of negotiation impasses or both. Such techniques should be utilized only pursuant to a specific agreement on a particular impasse between the department or agency and a labor organization granted exclusive recognition and should be resorted to only after other available techniques have been used. The agreement should establish a defined set of issues that will be subject to fact finding or arbitration and should provide that the costs incurred be shared.

While a variety of impasse-resolving techniques including fact finding and arbitration should be made available, the Committee strongly believes that fact finding or arbitration should be resorted to only after earnest efforts by the parties to reach agreement through direct negotiations and after referral to higher authority within the department or agency and the national office of the labor organization. To assure that the availability of fact finding or arbitration is not resorted to prematurely, the approval of the agency head and, where appropriate, i.e., in conformity with internal labor organization procedure, the national office of the labor organization, should be obtained. The recommendations or awards should be accepted in the same manner as in the arbitration of grievances and appeals and should be subject to challenge only on grounds similar to those discussed in that section of this report.

While it is anticipated that voluntary techniques should resolve most negotiation impasses, the Committee recognizes that there may be situations where, despite the efforts of the parties, a settlement may not be reached. In such cases, either or both parties should have the right to request the services of the Federal Labor Relations Panel, subject to such necessary rules as it may prescribe. Thereupon, the Panel should have the authority to (1) review the efforts made by the parties to reach agreement; (2) determine the nature of the unresolved matter (s) ; (3) suggest other voluntary methods that could be utilized; and (4) decide, after consideration of the views of the parties, whether the impasse is of such nature that it is appropriate to assert jurisdiction. Upon determination that it should exercise jurisdiction, the Panel should have the authority to determine whether to submit the matter to an expert or panel of experts from within or outside of the Federal service for recommendations to the Panel which in turn would issue a final and binding decision to the agency head and organization and publish such decision in the Federal Register. In special circumstances, the Panel may decide to hear the matter itself. The costs of proceedings should be shared by the parties.

STATE LAWS [4]

The spread of work stoppages involving public employees, particularly in local government, has stirred a renewed interest in approaches to dealing with these situations. The prevailing legal view that public employees do not and should not have the right to strike has not changed over the years. But the approaches to the problem of handling such strikes when they occur have changed—from demanding punitive measures to advocating rightful opportunities for government employees to form labor organizations and obtain their recognition, while providing alternative approaches to strike-inducing impasses.

The change in attitude is the product of slow but steady development at Federal, state, and local levels. The pressing need has been to provide government employees with avenues, comparable to those available to workers in the private sector, for expressing their views on the conditions under which they work and for safeguarding their common interests. . . .

The sources of experience in dealing with the problems of organization, representation, and collective bargaining for public employees have been limited, and largely of recent origin. The traditional view in law and judicial decisions has been that government could not negotiate with its employees, for this would involve a diminution of its sovereignty. Strikes of public employees have almost universally been considered illegal, and this view remains largely unaltered even as avenues for negotiation have been provided by law or administrative action.

[4] From "Labor-Management Relations Laws in Public Service," by Joseph P. Goldberg, special assistant to the Commissioner of Labor Statistics, Bureau of Labor Statistics, United States Department of Labor. *Monthly Labor Review.* 91:48-55. Je. '68.

Public employees were specifically excluded from the coverage of the National Labor Relations Act and its amendments. The Taft-Hartley Act banned strikes by Federal employees, with the penalty of automatic discharge and a three-year ban on reemployment for the violators. Several state laws in the early post-World War II years also provided for automatic discharge of strikers with opportunity for reemployment only after one to three years' suspension, and then only at the salary at which discharge had occurred. The most prominent example was the New York State's Condon-Wadlin Act, of which Governor Rockefeller said in signing its successor [the Taylor Law], "The necessity of this [new] law has unquestionably been demonstrated over the years by utter inadequacy of the Condon-Wadlin Law to resolve paralyzing strikes and threats of strikes by public employees."

The other avenue to experience has been that available to employees in private enterprise who, where subject to Federal jurisdiction, enjoy the right to organize and bargain collectively as provided by the Labor Management Relations Act. Further, one third of the states have enacted labor relations acts to provide like opportunities and procedures for employees of private enterprises subject only to state jurisdiction. As the problems of labor relations in public employment grew, several cities, notably New York and Philadelphia, developed machinery to deal with their employees. The states increasingly accorded, by statute, administrative action, and judicial decision, their employees the right to organize and to confer with public employers. The means for regularizing such arrangements through representation elections, bargaining procedures, and impasse-breaking measures remained to be developed.

A landmark was set by the enactment of the Wisconsin Municipal Employee Relations Act in 1959, which conferred on municipal employees the right to organize and negotiate with their employers. Even greater impetus to employee organization and state action was generated by the Federal Government's Executive Order 10988, issued by President

Kennedy in 1962. . . . [See "Executive Order 10988," in this section, above.]

Approaches to Legislation

The altered climate for public employee relations in recent years has been evidenced by the establishment of Federal, state, and local commissions to examine trends and experience, with recommendations for new or amended legislation. Most notable, of course, was the 1961 report of the President's Task Force on Employee-Management Relations in the Federal Service, whose recommendations formed the basis for Executive Order 10988.

Similar use of study committees by a number of state and local governments has provided extensive background and considered recommendations which have been incorporated in statutes (Connecticut, Minnesota, New York State, New York City, Rhode Island) or provided bases for ongoing discussions on legislation (Illinois and Michigan) . . . .

All of the reports have stressed the need for regularization of the means whereby organizations of public employees may be given an opportunity to obtain representation, to represent the employees of the appropriate unit in the determination of their working conditions and in effectuating the agreement, and to provide the devices for avoiding impasse situations that impede agreement. They have viewed such arrangements as enhancing the merit system, not as conflicting with it.

Cited prominently was the importance of adequate training in techniques of negotiation and contract administration for both public management and public employee representatives, so as to ensure good faith bargaining and observance of agreements as integral to the regular operations of the agencies covered. In making statutory recommendations, the reports stressed open-mindedness and flexibility in this new field, with continuing assessment of initial experience, so that the law and its administration could be improved. . . .

State Law Trends

Since the enactment of the 1959 Wisconsin Municipal Employee Relations Act, legislation in some dozen states has included comprehensive statutes authorizing or requiring public employers to recognize and negotiate with organizations chosen by their employees, and generally provided for fact finding in the event of impasses. In most other states, employees are accorded—by statute, executive order, or administrative action—the right to organize, and in many instances their organizations have the right to present proposals and grievances. In a number of states where comprehensive legislation with broad public employee covering is lacking, statutes have been enacted authorizing union recognition or establishing fact-finding procedures or both, for such special occupational groups viewed as intimately concerned with the public interest as firefighters, policemen, transit system employees and nurses. Only Texas and Virginia statutes specifically forbid bargaining with public employee unions, and only North Carolina and Alabama statutes specifically forbid state employees from joining unions.

Laws extending representation arrangements to broad groups of public employees have been enacted since 1959 in Wisconsin, Connecticut, California, Delaware, Massachusetts, Michigan, Minnesota, Missouri, Nebraska, New York, Oregon, Rhode Island, Vermont, and Washington. Other states during this period have enacted statutes granting the right to organize to all public employees, as in Iowa and Florida, or only to special groups, as to firefighters in Wyoming, nurses in Montana, or firemen and transit workers in Illinois. . . .

Scope. The statutes vary in their scope. Some include all local and state employees, others cover municipal employees, often excluding or separating teachers and covering them by other laws. Special provisions for policemen and firemen may be made in a more inclusive law, or may be included in separate statutes.

Administrative Machinery. Only in New York has a new Public Employment Relations Board been established, an autonomous unit within the State Civil Service Commission, dealing with both representation and impasse situations. [See "New York's Taylor Law" and "New York PERB in Action," in this section, below.] However, under this statute, local authorities are authorized to establish their own representation procedures if they meet the state's requirements. Generally, the existing machinery for mediation and for determining employee representation for collective bargaining relationships in private enterprise has been used. Some statutes leave administrative machinery to local authorities, particularly for teachers.

Bargaining. Most statutes require mandatory bargaining by the public employer with public employee organizations and execution of written agreements (Connecticut, Massachusetts, Missouri, New York, Rhode Island, Wisconsin, and Michigan). Bargaining is mandatory for state and county employees, but only permissive for municipal employees, under the Delaware statute, and the Vermont statute's coverage of city employees is permissive. The mandatory right "to meet and confer" is accorded all covered employees in Minnesota and California. In Washington and Oregon, mandatory bargaining is required for state and local employees, while the mandatory right to "meet and confer" is accorded to teachers.

Where machinery is established for representation, mediation, and fact finding, existing state agencies are usually utilized. Existing labor relations boards are utilized for both representation and mediation situations in Michigan and Wisconsin. Where separate labor relations boards and mediation agencies are established, the functions of representation determination and mediation are separated, as in Connecticut, Massachusetts, and Rhode Island. The state department of labor is utilized in Delaware, Minnesota, and Vermont, the mediation board in Missouri, and civil service commissions in Oregon and Washington. In Wisconsin, however, the state director of personnel has the function of representing the state as employer.

The special statutes for teachers generally leave to local school boards the determination of representation and mediation procedures. Mediation services under these laws are generally provided by the state department of education. Under the Rhode Island teacher statute, representation certifications are made by the labor relations board.

Representation Status. Almost all of the recent statutes requiring bargaining provide machinery for the election and certification of employee organizations, with exclusive representation rights. Minnesota grants a formal status to organizations with a majority status, and informal status to other groups, with the right to meet and confer. The teachers' statutes, as in the case of Connecticut and Washington, require local boards to establish procedures for determining the majority status for representation purposes. In California and Minnesota, where more than one organization represents the teachers, provision is made for employee organization councils based on proportionate representation.

Negotiations, Impasses, and Strikes. The statutes of all the states with recent legislation on government employees (except California) contain varying provisions on negotiations and disputes. Characteristically, some of those measures outline guides on negotiations, with due consideration to timing as regards budgetary determinations. On inability to conclude agreements, a provision is made for mediation and fact finding by state boards and for nonbinding recommendations, notably in the case of Connecticut, Massachusetts, Michigan, Minnesota, and Wisconsin. Recourse to state mediation services is provided in the Delaware and Rhode Island statutes. The Rhode Island and Vermont statutes provide for efforts to obtain agreement on voluntary arbitration. Strikes are specifically prohibited in most of the statutes. Generally, sanctions are not set forth specifically, leaving actions deemed necessary by the public authorities to be taken through the courts.

STATE LAWS—RECENT CHANGES [5]

Important improvements or new legislation affecting the rights of employees in public and private employment were enacted [in 1968] by a number of states. New Jersey created a Public Employment Relations Commission charged with the regulation of employer-employee relations in public employment, particularly as regards dispute settlement and grievance procedures.

The Territory of Guam, in enacting a comprehensive modern labor code to meet its changing labor scene, passed . . . a Public Employee-Management Relations Act for government employees. . . .

Other new laws gave the right to organize and bargain collectively: to public school employees in Maryland, but prohibited strikes by such employees; to local transportation authorities in Delaware, with a provision for binding arbitration and a strike prohibition; to public employees in Chatham County and the City of Savannah, Georgia, permitting checkoff of union dues; and to policemen and firemen of political subdivisions in Pennsylvania, with provision for binding arbitration.

A 1961 California law granting public employees the right to organize and requiring public agencies to confer with their unions was strengthened by a provision (not applicable to state employees) for mediation of disputes. The amendment also called for mutual consultation in the development of rules and regulations for the administration of employer-employee relations. Delaware set up collective bargaining procedures for its state employees, and Maine provided for a governor-appointed State Employees Appeals Board empowered to mediate and arbitrate grievances and disputes between individual employees and their agencies— except for issues of classification and pay. Massachusetts

[5] From "Review of State Labor Laws Enacted in 1968," by Clara T. Sorenson, labor standards adviser, Bureau of Labor Statistics, United States Department of Labor. *Monthly Labor Review*. 92:41-6. Ja. '69.

made it mandatory for housing authorities to bargain collectively and sign agreements with their employees. . . .

Amendments to two states' labor relations acts extended collective bargaining protection to formerly exempt employees—in Massachusetts, to nonprofessional employees in public or private health care facilities, and in New York, to employees of nonprofit charitable, educational, and religious organizations.

NEW YORK'S TAYLOR LAW [6]

Beginnings under a new law are often difficult and complex, requiring the establishment of an entirely new agency to administer the statute as well as the promulgation of rules and regulations under which the statute is implemented and enforced.

On September 1, 1967, when the Taylor Law went into effect, the New York State Public Employment Relations Board, the agency established to administer the Law, found itself faced immediately with a number of major problems, among which were:

> Defining the nature, role and responsibilities of the Board
>
> Adoption of rules and regulations to implement the Law
>
> Clarifying the options available to local governments under Section 212 of the Law, including the establishment of their own public employment relations boards
>
> Developing an organizational pattern, hiring and training employees, and securing necessary funds for the administration of the agency, and
>
> Informing public employers, public employees, employee organizations, and the public of a com-

[6] From *Year One of the Taylor Law, September 1, 1967-August 31, 1968.* New York State Public Employment Relations Board. 875 Central Ave. Albany, N.Y. 12206. '68. p 4-17. Reprinted by permission.

plex new law and a new way of life for those in the
public sector

From the outset, the PERB recognized that for the Taylor
Law to be effective, the Board must be neutral and impartial.
The Board charted such a course and followed it.

The state Public Employment Relations Board was created under Section 205 of the Taylor Law. The Board consists of three members, appointed by the governor. Not more
than two members of the Board may be members of the
same political party. Board members are appointed for six-
year terms. The chairman of the Board is the only full-time
member. The other two members are paid on a per diem
basis. In addition to the Board's statutory responsibility for
resolving disputes arising out of contract negotiations, and
promulgating rules to implement the intent of the Taylor
Law regarding representation questions, the Board serves in
a quasi-judicial role in determining whether employee organizations violate the no-strike provision of the statute.

The Board also sits as an appellant, hearing appeals
from decisions of the director of representation. The Board
is the policy-making body for the administration of the Law.

The chairman of the Board serves as the chief administrative officer, in addition to other responsibilities, for the
day-to-day operations.

There are some 90,000 public employees in New York
State working for the state, municipalities, counties, towns,
villages, school districts and public authorities. In the first
year, 1967-68, more than 700,000 public employees were represented by employee organizations in collective negotiations
with their employers.

About 340,000 of these public employees gained recognition and engaged in some form of negotiations with their
public employers prior to the enactment of the Taylor Law,
and most of these were in New York City. An estimated
360,000 obtained and are now exercising such rights for the
first time. Thousands more are in various stages of obtaining
representation rights.

Most public employers, and public employee organizations seeking to represent employees, have avoided disputes over representation questions. In fact, most representation disputes were resolved either under the auspices of local procedures established to resolve such disputes or voluntarily without resort to such procedures. Preliminary indications show that recognitions have been granted to employee organizations by at least two hundred local governments outside of New York City, and not including school districts.

In the school districts, recognition was extended to employee organizations representing professional employees (mostly classroom teachers) in some 600 districts out of a total of more than 800 operating districts.

The great majority of these recognitions were granted since the effective date of the Taylor Law. Employee organizations representing police and firemen have achieved recognition in most of the governments likely to have public safety agencies.

In addition to the large number of voluntary recognitions, the services of the PERB were used to settle 164 representation disputes [in the first year], and all without resort to strike. . . .

Significant Decisions

A number of significant unit determination decisions were issued by the director of representation and the Board.

The most far-reaching of these cases in terms of the number of employees involved and the issues raised is the "general unit" designated by the state for all employees except those in the Division of New York State Police, the professional staff of the State University and those defined as management or confidential. The unit determination question for these employees is generally regarded as one of the most complex labor relations matters of its kind, in either public or private employment. Over 3,700 different job titles are held by the 150,000 state employees in the "general unit."

More than fifty petitions were filed with PERB contesting the state's unit decision, and its recognition of the Civil Service Employees' Association as negotiating agent. As a preliminary action in this case, a request was made to the Board to order the state's negotiating team to cease negotiations with the CSEA in the general unit. After hearings on this issue, the Board ordered the state to treat all competing organizations equally in the negotiations until such time as a final determination could be made on the merits of the representation question by PERB. The Court of Appeals, however, in a 5-2 decision, ruled that the Board did not have the authority to issue such an order.

Following nearly eight months of hearings, an intermediate determination was issued by the director of representation based on recommendations of the Board's deputy chairman who served as hearing officer in the case. That decision established six negotiating units as follows: Operational Services; Inspection and Security Services; Health Services and Support; Administrative Services; Professional, Scientific and Technical Services; and Seasonal Employees of the Long Island State Park Commission. Appeals were filed from this decision with the state PERB by the state and eleven of the employee organizations that had contested the state's original unit determination. The state PERB is responsible for making the final unit determination. [See the following article.] . . .

Determinations in all representation disputes before PERB were made on the facts of the case and at times resulted in different determinations from area to area for members of a similar profession. To illustrate, in two early cases classroom teachers were placed in a separate unit from principals and in a later case, both groups were consolidated in one unit.

The question of placement of technical and professional and supervisory employees was one of the principal issues in another major unit determination affecting employees of the New York State Thruway. At issue, also, was the placement of office clericals and bridge painters. Here, the director of representation attempted to resolve the dispute by establishing two units, one for all toll collectors, maintenance and clerical employees and the other for all technical, professional and supervisory employees. Three of the four employee organizations competing for representation rights appealed this decision to the PERB.

Each situation at the present state of development of the law presents new, unusual and distinct problems calling for critical and in-depth analysis of the facts. . . .

In summary, the representation machinery provided under the Taylor Law appears to be working well. Not only are thousands of employees being represented in negotiations by employee organizations, but most importantly there have been no strikes involving representation issues. The Taylor Law is fulfilling one of its primary objectives: giving employees the right to choose an employee organization, and to negotiate collectively on terms and conditions of employment. Indeed, it was a large order for a new statute.

The Taylor Law is unique in public employment in that, for the first time, it establishes impasse procedures for the resolution of public employer-employee disputes that arise out of contract negotiations.

Section 209 of the Taylor Law provides that public employers and recognized or certified employee organizations may enter into written agreements setting forth procedures to be invoked if disputes arise during the course of collective negotiations. These written agreements may be incorporated in a broader, collectively negotiated contract or may be separate written agreements for the limited purpose of resolving particular disputes. If agreed-upon machinery for resolving disputes breaks down, or if the parties fail to agree on such procedures, then the state Public Employment Relations Board is obliged to invoke the Taylor Law's impasse procedures.

As one of its first tasks, even prior to the implementation of the law, the state board actively contacted public employee organizations and public employers to develop a panel of mediators and fact finders. By the close of the year, 160 experienced labor relations people were named to the panel and were being used effectively throughout the state.

Under the mutually agreed-upon impasse procedures permitted by the statute, the parties to a dispute have unlimited flexibility in establishing machinery that best meets their needs. A problem, however, arises when such machinery fails to resolve a dispute and state PERB is summoned, usually with only a few days, and sometimes only hours, available before a contract expires or budgets are to be submitted. (The PERB is analyzing cases of this type in an effort to devise an approach that retains the flexibility for the parties, . . . [and] at the same time will permit PERB's intervention, if the dispute continues, with sufficient time to be of most help.)

The first major round of negotiations under the law's impasse machinery has been completed. From September 1, 1967, through August 30, 1968, the Conciliation Section of the Board handled in excess of three hundred contract disputes in governmental entities ranging from large cities to tiny fire districts, as well as in school districts of all sizes throughout the state. By far, disputes between teacher organizations and local school boards exceeded all others.

Approximately 80 per cent of the disputes involved school boards and their employees. Boards of education negotiated with employees in over 1,600 negotiating units. PERB was involved in 226 disputes arising from these negotiations. Two developments were noticeable in school negotiations. The first was the extent of the Board's involvement, clearly greater than that of private sector mediation agencies; secondly, over 50 per cent of the disputes which came to the Board were settled through mediation.

The first major dispute handled by the Board involved the Triborough Bridge and Tunnel Authority and Local 1396, American Federation of State, County and Municipal Employees, AFL-CIO. This was the first instance of full application of the impasse procedures. A PERB staff conciliator

was assigned; a mediator was appointed, and the first fact-
finding panel was appointed by PERB. The recommendations of the panel were accepted by the employer and the
employee organizations and settled the dispute. The case
clearly demonstrated that competent fact finding, with equitable recommendations, can be an effective tool in the total
impasse machinery.

The effectiveness of the law's impasse machinery was
manifested in numerous other disputes, but perhaps none
more so than in the contract dispute between the Plainview-
Old Bethpage School district in the Town of Oyster Bay, and
the Federation of Teachers. Here, a three-man fact-finding
board, assigned following mediation efforts, held marathon
hearings over a weekend and resolved 120 issues, thus avert-
ing a strike set for the next day.

A landmark in the implementation of the law's impasse
provisions involved a dispute between the City of Schenec-
tady and the Patrolmen's Benevolent Association and Local
28 of the Fire Fighters Union.

The city challenged PERB's authority to enter a contract
dispute after the budget submission date and brought the
matter to the Supreme Court. In his decision, a Supreme
Court Justice upheld the state board's right to invoke its impasse machinery despite the budget date. The judge stated
in part: "It is apparent . . . that the legislature intended
PERB to possess powers and duties necessary to give the Taylor Law meaning." He also said: "In order to effectuate the
Law the section on impasse machinery must be given a construction which does not render PERB powerless when an
impasse does in fact exist."

While PERB's role was paramount in resolving the three
hundred impasses that came to it directly, the Board also
was in close touch with other labor relations crises where
negotiations were carried on under procedures established
by parties to the dispute.

The state board was actively involved in negotiations between the New York City Transit Authority and the Trans-

port Workers' Union from initial discussions early in October 1967 up to the settlement two hours beyond the strike deadline. Under Section 209 of the Taylor Law, the TA and the TWU selected to establish their own procedures and named a three-man mediation panel. The Board remained in continuous contact through the marathon bargaining sessions in the event negotiations broke down and the full impasse procedures of the Taylor Law would have to be invoked.

In still another case, also involving New York City's subway system, the state PERB was able to effect a settlement between the Transit Authority and three supervisory unions. Unique in this case was PERB's implementation of the broad statutory authority vested in it to resolve disputes. PERB introduced for the first time under the Taylor Law the "show cause" hearing in which the parties to the dispute were permitted to give evidence on the question of why a fact finder's recommendations should not be accepted.

The relationship between PERB and the OCB [New York City Office of Collective Bargaining] was given considerable attention by the Taylor Committee when it was reconvened by the governor following the sanitationmen's strike. The Taylor Law virtually assures complete autonomy to OCB, except that its procedures may be challenged in the Supreme Court in New York City. [See "The Need for Legislative Action" in this section, above.] . . .

The overall picture for Year One was bright despite the fact that nine strikes occurred. During the first year time did not always permit the full use of the impasse machinery of the Taylor Law. Rather than taking advantage of the mediation step of the impasse procedures, in many instances it was necessary to proceed directly to fact finding. In the future, however, as experience grows, the state board anticipates earlier contact with the parties to disputes to insure full use of the law's dispute-settling machinery.

[Amendments to the Taylor Law were enacted in 1969 to increase penalties for unions and employees engaged in a strike; to specify improper practices of governmental employers and unions; and to provide additional procedures when a negotiations impasse is reached. These and other changes are detailed in an appendix to "New York Public Employee Relations Laws," by H. H. Rains (*Labor Law Journal*. 20:264-88. My. '69).—Ed.]

NEW YORK PERB IN ACTION [7]

The [1969] runaway victory won by the old-line Civil Service Employees Association in elections to pick bargaining representatives for 137,000 New York State employees is a repudiation at the state level of the kind of militant tactics that have kept New York City's relations with its unionized public workers in perpetual turmoil.

The independent association, which devoted much of its energy in past years to functioning as an insurance agency for state employees, decisively defeated the more aggressive American Federation of State, County and Municipal Employees in all but the smallest of the five negotiating units established by the Public Employment Relations Board. The outcome makes the CSEA the dominant pattern-setter in wage negotiations and greatly reduces the danger that the state will be subjected to interunion whipsawing of the type that has proved so costly to this city.

The strikes its AFL-CIO rival called in state mental hospitals ... [in the fall of 1968] to dramatize charges that Governor Rockefeller was giving the association preferred treatment undoubtedly boomeranged; their impact on the election sentiment of the great mass of state workers appears to have been negative. ...

New York State's experience ought to persuade states that still have no orderly machinery for determining union representation of the desirability for creating such machinery. That would obviate such harsh community battles over

[7] From "Less Chaos in Public Service," editorial. New York *Times*. p 34. Ag. 11, '69. © 1969 by The New York Times Company. Reprinted by permission.

union recognition as attended the unionization of Memphis sanitation workers and Charleston, South Carolina, hospital employees.

The results of the state voting should also help convince the strike-prone leaders of New York City's civil service unions that it is past time to abandon policies that substitute economic force for lawful process in contract disputes with the city.

Evidence that this realization may finally be sinking in is provided by the reported willingness of the labor members of the Municipal Labor Committee to join Mayor Lindsay and the public members in recommending that procedures for final and binding determination of disputes be incorporated in new state legislation covering the city's Office of Collective Bargaining.

The Mayor is right in believing that all 300,000 municipal employees, including those in such agencies as the Transit Authority and the Board of Education, ought to be brought within the scope of a uniform machinery for maintaining labor peace and equity. His proposals will give pause to many traditionalists in both government and organized labor, but they represent a realistic road to greater stability as well as justice in municipal employee relations.

VI. PUBLIC UNIONISM ABROAD

EDITOR'S INTRODUCTION

Other countries have quite different views on public employee unionism. Canada, as John W. Henley describes it, is experimenting with various approaches among the various provinces. The lack of total success in these methods is highlighted by Montreal's brief but terrifying experience in a police and firemen's strike, as described in the second article. The British and continental experience, as the next two articles indicate, concentrates at both ends of the spectrum—from strict regulation and strike prohibition to general acceptance of bargaining and strikes by public employees. In the final selection W. A. Pullan presents a British view of how to conduct labor relations on a local level through mutual understanding and patience rather than elaborate legal devices.

Proponents of almost any opinion on public sector collective bargaining in the United States can find support in the widely varying experiences reviewed in this section, yet obvious benefit is to be derived from a study of legislation and attitudes abroad.

THE CANADIAN EXPERIENCE [1]

To understand the Canadian experience [in public sector bargaining] one must first of all consider the nature of labor relations jurisdiction in Canada. In contrast to the United States, federal jurisdiction is very limited indeed. It is expressed in a federal statute, the Industrial Relations Disputes Investigation Act, which applies to employers and employees

[1] From address by John W. Henley, vice president—personnel, Canadian Westinghouse Company Limited, before the American Management Association Personnel Conference, New York City, February 4, 1969. The author. Hamilton, Ontario. '69. p 2-6. Reprinted by permission.

connected with the operation of any work within the legislative authority of the Parliament of Canada. This includes railways, seaways, telegraphs, radio stations and Crown corporations.

You will note from this that federal government law and practices have little do to with the private sector of the economy. Only a handful of Crown-owned corporations engaged in manufacturing and a number of companies engaged in interprovincial transportation and some other services are subject to federal law in labor relations. . . .

The ten Canadian provinces . . . all have statutory law, most commonly entitled the Labour Relations Act, governing labor relations in all parts of the private sector.

While the provincial statutes can and do vary considerably in detail, there are two conditions common to almost all of them, which are also to be found in the federal statute and both of which distinguish the Canadian scene from the American scene:

First of all, there is statutory prohibition of strikes during the life of collective agreements. The province of Saskatchewan is an exception here.

Secondly, strike action is not legal until government-imposed mediation procedures have been complied with and exhausted.

We believe that both of these provisions, despite their imperfections and the breaches which do occur, and despite the excesses of the last few inflationary years, have served the country well.

Turning now to legislation affecting public service employees (and by these I mean employees of provincial governments) , we find a rather mixed bag: In some provinces there is separate and special legislation while in others public service employees come under the Labour Relations Act. In still others, there is no legislation at all, except for exclusion from the provincial Labour Relations Act.

If there can be said to be a typical situation at all in provincial jurisdiction it is about as follows and the Province of Ontario, neighbor to New York State, Ohio, and Michigan would be representative:

First, a Labour Relations Act governing employment in the private sector and often employment in the municipal segment of the public sector and conferring a right to strike.

Secondly, a Public Service Act or a Civil Service Act governing provincial government employees, i.e. civil servants. There may or may not be a right to strike: At the present time provincial government employees may strike in at least three out of ten jurisdictions.

Thirdly, there is an array of other special statutes such as in Ontario, for example, where there is separate legislation covering policemen, firemen and hospital employees under which strikes are prohibited and arbitration of disputes is compulsory.

Public service employees who are civil servants of the federal government are governed by the Public Service Staff Relations Act, first enacted in March 1967. This act regulates labor relations bargaining units in federal jurisdiction and contains a provision under which bargaining units prior to the commencement of bargaining must opt for the right to strike or to accept arbitration. That provision of the statute conferring a right to strike was strongly opposed by management groups throughout the country but was passed by the Pearson Liberal government which then lacked a majority in the House of Commons and was dependent on opposition party support for its survival, including from time to time support from Canada's Socialists, the New Democratic Party, which in turn derives major financial support from the Canadian Labour Congress (the counterpart organization of your AFL-CIO) through union dues checked off by management.

To date, under the Public Service Staff Relations Act, only eight bargaining units out of sixty-eight have opted for the right to strike. But statistics don't tell the full story: Those opting for the right to strike include such groups as nonsupervisory postal employees, air traffic controllers, radio operators, supervisory and nonsupervisory ship repairers, nonsupervisory ships crews, supervisory and nonsupervisory printers.

Moreover, those who originally opted for compulsory arbitration rather than the right to strike have the further right to reverse that decision on each occasion when their contract expires!

If this description has confused you in some measure, it will also serve to emphasize that there is no single system of industrial relations in Canada, nor, in my opinion is one likely to develop. Confusing as this situation can be, it also has its strengths and provides a laboratory for some experiment without the attendant perils of experimentation involving nationwide impact.

In still other situations, unions for public service employees, instead of outright strike, have resorted to "work-to-rule" campaigns. . . .

If there is one single lesson to be learned from the Canadian experience it is this: Whatever the pressures, political or other, do not affirm or enshrine in legislation a right to strike for civil servants. It is difficult to find any other national jurisdiction where such right has been affirmed in statute. It must be put down as a monumental error of the Liberal government in Canada and it will not be easy to retrieve. The Winnipeg *Free Press* has stated it editorially as follows:

> In practical politics it will be difficult for the Trudeau government to repeal the mistake of its predecessor without seeming hostile to labor in general, though such criticism misses the whole point of the argument and the special status of public employees. By the nature of their work they cannot be allowed to use the strike weapons used by unions in private industry if the state is to function as the final protector of society. . . .

Our official tolerance of strikes in the public sector, whether under law as in Canada, or *de facto* as in the United States *and* Canada, is threatening to undermine the basis of free collective bargaining in the private sector. In Canada it is always more than a threat....

Strikes are intolerable in themselves when they exist in the public sector. And it must be our objective to remove the strike weapon from employees of all tax-supported institutions with realistic sanctions to ensure observance. The continuance of such strikes, legal or illegal, is a serious enough threat to order in society. But continuance means even more: In seeking to control strikes the public and our legislators may fail to make proper distinction between the public and private sectors, and since all major strikes are inconvenient and disruptive, end up by banning many private sector strikes. If that development ensues, then we will no longer preserve the free market economy we have known.

It follows that business management must address itself to the problems of collective bargaining in the public sector or face its demise in the private sector.

THE CANADIAN SYSTEM BREAKS DOWN [2]

Montrealers discovered . . . [in October 1969] what it is like to live in a city without police and firemen. The lesson was costly: six banks were robbed, more than one hundred shops were looted, and there were twelve fires. Property damage came close to $3 million; at least forty carloads of glass will be needed to replace shattered storefronts. Two men were shot dead. At that, Montreal was probably lucky to escape as lightly as it did.

The immediate cause of the outburst was a strike for more pay staged by the city's cops and firemen. There were far deeper causes as well. The happy glow cast by Expo 67 has faded. Separatists advocating an independent Quebec have ignited a series of violent demonstrations and bomb explosions. A continuing fiscal crisis—caused in part by the heavy expenses of keeping a section of Expo open—has alien-

[2] From "City Without Cops." Time. 94:47. O. 17, '69. Copyright Time Inc. 1969. Reprinted by permission.

ated Montrealers from their political leaders. The city's police were particularly angry because their Toronto counterparts receive more pay for less dangerous work. When the city offered the police an increase that still left them $800 short of Toronto's basic $9,200-a-year scale, the cops struck. As an Ottawa official put it: "The people who had been kicking them and stoning them and bashing them over the head weren't paying them enough for it." ...

[On October 7] the 8 A.M. police shift went off to the Paul Sauvé Arena to argue strike tactics instead of reporting to their beats. Suddenly the city was left unguarded. By 11:20 A.M., the first bank robbery had occurred. By noon shops began to close, and banks shut their doors to all except old customers. Early in the evening, a group of taxi drivers added to the confusion. Protesting the fact that they are prohibited from serving Montreal's airport, they led a crowd of several hundred to storm the garage of the Murray Hill Limousine Service Ltd., which has the lucrative franchise. Buses were overturned and set ablaze. From nearby rooftops, snipers' shots rang out. A handful of frightened Quebec provincial police, called in to help maintain order, stood by helplessly. One was shot in the back by a sniper and died.

The crowd, augmented by other opportunists, moved through downtown Montreal, burning and looting. Rioters stormed into the swanky Queen Elizabeth Hotel, then moved on to the nearby Windsor Hotel and nearly wrecked Mayor Jean Drapeau's newly opened restaurant. Expensive shops along St. Catherine's Street were hit by looters. On the city's outskirts, burglars went to work; one was shot dead by a doctor in his suburban home.

Belatedly, the Quebec provincial government called out 600 infantrymen and 300 Royal Canadian Mounted Police. It also rammed through an emergency law ordering police and firemen back to duty by midnight under threat of heavy penalties, including fines of up to $100 a day per striker. Soon after midnight, the cops began reappearing, made more than sixty arrests.

To Prime Minister Pierre Trudeau, the trouble in Montreal was "part of a total society which is running amok. . . . I am not saying the upsurge of violence is a Montreal phenomenon. It is a modern-day phenomenon." On Montreal's Black Tuesday, however, it was a relatively small band of thugs, militant students and separatists that caused most of the damage. Only when the looting began did other, less committed opportunists join in. Ordinary citizens amused themselves chiefly by running red lights—but nothing more.

THE EUROPEAN EXPERIENCE [3]

For those who are inclined to resist public employee unionism in the United States, or believe its scope can or should be restricted to implementing civil service rules and laws, I suggest that European experience indicates an evolutionary perspective. More and more public employees are likely to be drawn into unionism and collective bargaining. Furthermore, the scope of issues falling within the bargaining relationship is also likely to expand, if European experience is any guide to the future of the United States in this respect. For example, under present circumstances in the United States at the Federal level, and even in many state and local situations, the possibility that the legislature will give up its general wage setting power over most civil servants seems somewhat remote. This has, however, come about in most of Europe, and I do not believe the United States is likely to be an exception. . . .

The process whereby civil service bargaining in Europe came to embrace more and more substantive issues, such as the determination of wages and hours has often entailed the passage of a special piece of enabling legislation (or a special governmental order or decree). This has been true even in countries where private sector bargaining has usually had

[3] From "Public Employee Bargaining in Europe," an excerpt adapted from a paper by Everett M. Kassalow, professor of economics, University of Wisconsin, presented to the 21st annual winter meeting of the Industrial Relations Research Association, December 1968. *Monthly Labor Review*. 92:47-9. Mr. '69.

only an informal base, with little or no support in legislation.

Despite the traditional emphasis upon voluntary, informal relations procedures and methods in Sweden and Great Britain, both these countries found it necessary and desirable to establish more secure systems of bargaining for civil servants. Both governments have also gone far in defining the scope of bargaining for civil servants, and have established rather formal procedures for union recognition.

In a number of other continental European countries, such bargaining rights as civil servants enjoy often derive from the simple provision in the national constitution guaranteeing the rights of all citizens to form trade unions. In most countries these rights, as they have come to be applied to civil servants, have not yet embraced the right to negotiate a written collective agreement.

One clear lesson to be learned from the European experience is that there is no definite answer to the critically important question of whether there should or can be the right to strike in the public sector. One can find instances where unions and managers have decided to dispense with the strike and substituted alternative procedures for all dispute settlements in the public sector. In other countries, the clear right to strike available in the private sector has been transferred almost bodily into the public sector. Moreover, in both systems (as well as under variations of both which can also be found in Europe), unions and governments have, in most instances, developed a constructive relationship, with few work interruptions in the form of authorized or unauthorized strikes.

In several countries the right to strike is seemingly provided for all citizens by the national constitution. It is not always clear, however, that this right includes civil servants. For example, in Germany although the constitution provides trade union rights for everyone, and these are presumed to include the right to strike for workers, there appears to be general agreement among all parties that civil servants do not enjoy this right.

The general right to form unions under the French constitution, on the other hand, has led over time to the explicit acceptance of the right of civil servants to strike. A 1963 law allows civil servants' strikes, provided appropriate notice is furnished to the proper authority—at least five days before the strike—with information as to whether it is to be a strike of a limited or unlimited duration, the place, date, hour, etc.

In most continental European countries where the right to strike has been conceded, the government can usually draw upon a reserve power if a public employee strike lasts a considerable length of time. The drafting of strikers into military or national service, the use of the armed forces to man essential services—these and other devices have been resorted to on some occasions by the French and a few other governments when a civil service strike ceased to be of token character.

Generally speaking, certain types of employees such as police, firemen, or members of the armed services are forbidden to strike, by law or custom, in most countries.

Bargaining in Sweden

The special statute which establishes bargaining rights and procedures for Swedish civil servants, including the right to sign full-scale collective agreements, also grants the unequivocal right to strike. It was primarily to equalize the rights of civil servants with those enjoyed by workers in the private sector that the statute was enacted.

This act anticipates that strikes and lockouts in civil service bargaining may occur. Indeed, in 1966 a strike was called by a few sections of the teachers' union affiliated with the Central Organization of Swedish Professional Workers, one of the country's important labor federations. This strike call was followed shortly by the government's lockout order against the nonstriking teacher sections of the union. Such sharp action and tactics in generally peaceful Sweden created a crisis in the very first year of operations under the new civil servants bargaining statute.

To deal with the private sector's strikes which may "imperil the public interest," the leading Swedish labor federation and the Employers Confederation have a special procedure which refers the dispute to a permanent standing council on which each is equally represented. This council will render a decision in case of strikes, or threats of strikes, in disputes affecting any vital public interest.

In the public service a special State Employee Council, the counterpart of the special council in the private sector, performs a similar function. This council consists of eight members, four of whom are appointed by the state and four by the central trade union organizations. Its decisions are taken by simple majority vote.

This dependence on a joint union-management body, with the implicit assumption that strikes in essential services will be prevented by it, is typical of the voluntaristic character of Swedish industrial relations.

Arbitration in Britain

In Britain, on the other hand, where voluntarism, as in Sweden, has also been a hallmark of the industrial relations scene, public employees' union and management have accepted a system of arbitration to resolve unsettled disputes. Strikes are a "disciplinary offense," if not exactly illegal. Actually, it was the civil service unions who struggled for some years to compel the government finally to accept arbitration as the method to resolve unsettled disputes; this was accomplished in 1925. A special Civil Service Arbitration Tribunal renders decisions which, broadly speaking, are binding on both parties.

The tribunal's scope of action includes such matters as pay and allowances, weekly hours, and vacations. Cases brought before the tribunal are confined to whole "classes" of civil servants, and individual employees' pay or other disputes do not come before it. Individuals' or small groups' grievances are taken up by the union acting at the various ministry (or department) levels.

For American students and industrial relations practitioners, the character of the British civil service arbitration procedures is worth some special consideration. The fear commonly expressed by unions and management in the United States, that the very existence of an arbitration alternative will render collective bargaining on interest matters ineffective or sterile, with one party or the other always forcing the issue to arbitration, has been dealt with rather creatively by the British.

Negotiations leading up to any possible submission to arbitration are of two types, formal and informal. In the formal stages briefs are exchanged, and the various offers and counteroffers are "on the record." Generally, at some point, negotiations proceed to the informal stage where, presumably, the parties make last-ditch concessions to one another in order to settle their disputes.

If a case is not settled and is submitted to arbitration, the offers and positions revert to those that were on the table —on the record—in the formal stages only. Neither side can refer to the off-the-record negotiations in their pleas before the tribunal. It has not been unknown for an arbitration tribunal to make an award which one party or the other found considerably less favorable than its opponent had offered during the informal bargaining stages.

Again, if the tribunal, which includes representatives of the union and the government as well as a permanent chairman, fails to agree on a decision, the chairman may make an "umpire's award." In a few cases the chairman has awarded less than the government ministry had earlier offered the employees. This, too, acts as a pressure on the unions, for example, to pursue arbitration only as a last resort.

As a consequence of the procedure, with its elements of uncertainty, both the union or staff side, as it is generally called, and the management have come more and more to shy away from excessive dependence on the Arbitration Tribunal. It is only the rare case that goes to arbitration today.

The Swedish and British experiences, one with its emphasis upon full rights of negotiation and strike (and lockout), the other geared to a system of arbitration with no real right to strike, carry one general message for the United States. Dogmatic insistence that only a "free" system of civil service bargaining with full right to strike (and lockout), or its counterpoint that there can be no right of public employees to strike, both seem more ideological than realistic.

Neither Swedish nor British experience is directly applicable to our situation; both, however, suggest that there are at least several possible roads to pursue in this matter of impasse strikes. The commonly expressed official view that strikes are impossible in public employment is often as doctrinaire as that of some union spokesmen who hold that there can never be an effective alternative to the right to strike even in public employment.

PUBLIC EMPLOYEE STRIKES [4]

There is no fixed pattern abroad [in dealing with strikes by public workers]. Teachers' strikes . . . occur in France. Work stoppages by public servants also are commonplace in Italy. But they are almost unheard of in Britain and Germany.

Nearly everywhere, strong legal restraints are on the books to discourage strikes against governments.

Britain

Private industry in this Socialist country has been reeling under the most serious wave of strikes in years. Not so the public sector.

The key is found in an elaborate combination of legislation, negotiation and arbitration.

[4] From "What Other Countries Do About Strikes Against Public." *U.S. News & World Report.* 65:62-3. D. 30, '68.

Run down the list of public servants and you find this:

Policemen are prohibited by law from joining trade unions. They must sign contracts that forbid action endangering public safety—such as strikes.

Firemen can join unions, but traditionally avoid taking steps that could jeopardize public safety. Employees of state-owned utilities cannot strike in violation of contracts.

Teachers and other government employees theoretically can strike. But effective machinery for negotiation and arbitration has virtually ruled out this sort of action.

How does Britain deal with wage demands and grievances from police, firemen and other government employees?

In the case of Britain's 100,000 policemen, the issues are heard by a joint council made up of representatives from an officially sanctioned police federation and from municipal, county and London metropolitan police forces.

If the council fails to reach agreement, either side can submit the dispute to arbitration.

The idea is for the council to grant wage increases every two years to keep pay in line with comparable jobs in private industry. Sometimes it doesn't work. For instance, policemen recently sought a 10 per cent wage increase, but settled for slightly less in view of the Labour government's policy of wage restraint.

A police spokesman describes as unthinkable any form of action to achieve their demands.

No one, this spokesman insists, would employ the measures that the police of New York City have used—calling in sick and slowing down their work. As the spokesman put it: "The sense of duty among police in this country is too strong to allow anything like that."

Firemen here belong to a union with more militant leadership, but it has not resorted to strikes. . . .

Some 280,000 teachers threatened a "work to rules" campaign or selective strikes lasting one day. They want a pay raise of 20 per cent. Officials offered 7 per cent over two years.

Procedures for handling teachers' demands are similar to those for other government employees—ending in arbitration, if necessary.

Despite this new note of militancy in some groups of public workers, the tendency here is to avoid extreme actions that might alienate popular support. The aim is to get maximum publicity and public backing for grievances, while causing minimum disruption of essential services to the public.

France

"In France you have to strike before anything is done."

The labor expert who said this explained that public workers here have few arbitration procedures to turn to. Strikes, marches, meetings and lobbying in the National Assembly are the only recourses for most civil employees.

Except for policemen and firemen—who legally cannot strike—French civil servants have used those recourses.

With regularity, there have been public strikes, most of them short—one-hour to twenty-four-hour walkouts against railways, post offices, the Paris bus and subway systems, the gas and electricity services.

In general, the government has resisted demands by public workers for higher pay, comparable to wages paid workers in similar jobs in private industry.

Big exception to the government's general indifference came . . . [in May-June 1968] when its employees joined rioting students and strikers in private industry to protest against the government.

Walkouts over a three-week period crippled transportation, government administration, mail and telegraph, city sanitation and schools. Outcome of the strikes: a 10 per cent increase in pay across the board for public workers.

By law, workers in nationalized sectors must give five days' notice of a strike, and must say how long it is going to last.

Even then, the government holds the upper hand. It is empowered to order workers back to their jobs, although this was not done . . . [in the 1968 strikes].

Policemen are forbidden, under a 1948 law, to strike. There never has been a walkout by police, although there were demonstrations protesting working conditions in 1958 and 1967.

Firemen, in effect, cannot strike either.

Most teachers in France are public servants or are paid government-scaled salaries. However, they have their own unions and can and do strike for more pay and better teaching conditions. Teachers usually join in the national "civil-servant strikes."

Since the spring riots, a new militancy has risen among public workers in the wake of the successes they achieved.

For instance, late in October, suburban-train drivers in Paris called a surprise one-day strike—ignoring the law calling for five days' advance notice.

Germany

The possibility that police, firemen or teachers would ever walk out seems outlandish to most Germans. As a result, no responsible official seems to have considered what might be done under such circumstances.

Strikes of any kind are almost unheard of in this prosperous country; strikes by public employees, absolutely so.

Year after year, the total number of man-days lost in all kinds of work stoppages in West Germany is unbelievably low. In 1965, it was 48,520; the next year, 27,086. In Britain and France the figures ran into the millions each year.

Pay increases in West Germany generally more than keep pace with union demands, so there is little pressure for strikes. But the main reason public workers stay on their jobs is a mixture of restraining laws and custom.

Of 2.9 million public employees in the nation, 1.3 million are classified as *Beamten,* or upper-grade workers, and have no legal right to strike. Their pay and working conditions are regulated by legislation. The 1.6 million lower-grade workers legally could strike, but they have not done so.

It is conceivable that the civil servants could employ slowdown techniques to try to achieve demands. But even this technique has been used only once, in 1963, when postal workers felt they had a grievance. [However, in September 1969, brief wildcat strikes among public employees occurred in the midst of the German parliamentary election campaign. Whether this type of action will spread in the future remains to be seen.—Ed.]

Italy

Policemen, firemen, teachers and other civil servants all have struck here in Italy at one time or another.

Civil servants joined in a general strike as recently as December 4 [1968].

All the strikes are legal.

The Italian constitution says every Italian has a right to strike "within the limits fixed by legislation"—and hardly any limits have been set.

Only in a few cases where danger to life could be acute has antistrike legislation been placed on the books. For instance, a sailor cannot quit work while at sea, and an airline pilot cannot refuse to handle a plane in flight.

One redeeming feature of walkouts here is that they usually do not last long—twenty-four hours or so. The main reason is that workers cannot afford to stay out for prolonged periods.

LOCAL RELATIONS IN BRITAIN [5]

Although industrial discipline is not always of the best in the local government service, it is to the credit of all concerned that the million or so people employed by [local government] authorities seldom withdraw their labor.

This is not because local authorities' employees receive high wages; their average earnings come well down the list published in the Ministry of Labour *Gazette* and compare unfavorably with those paid in the manufacturing industries.

Having been engaged in staff administration for more than thirty years, I have reached the conclusion that there are a number of reasons for this comparatively peaceful state of affairs. The most important are:

1. Local authorities have, on the whole, built up for themselves a reputation as good employers who try to keep to the rules, and trade union officials recognize them as such.

2. The trade union officials associated with the local government services seem to be in closer touch with their members than some of their counterparts in industry and are therefore in a more favorable position to give effective help in damping down disputes before they reach dangerous dimensions.

3. Most local authority employees work in small groups and are not therefore so exposed to the influence of militant shop stewards, one word from whom can close a factory.

4. A high proportion of local government employees still possess a sense of responsibility towards their jobs and are reluctant to let down the public whom they serve.

5. Few council [local government] employees do repetitive work of the production belt [assembly line] type,

[5] From "Labour Relations in Local Government," by W. A. Pullan, editor, *Municipal Year Book*, and former establishment officer, Leicestershire, England. *Municipal and Public Services Journal* (London). 76:309+. F. 9, '68. Reprinted by permission.

and because there is a certain amount of variety in their jobs, they obtain more satisfaction from their work.

6. The disputes machinery in local government has stood the test of many years and is accepted by employers and trade unions as fair and speedy.

Much of the credit . . . must go to Edward Bishop, the former employers' secretary [permanent staff officer] of the northwestern provincial councils, who during the 1920s traveled the country persuading local authorities to participate in schemes for joint negotiation.

During the past forty years Mr. Bishop's initial efforts have been developed until pay, conditions and disputes in almost every sector of the local government service are capable of being settled round the table.

All that has been said so far represents the brighter side of the picture, but the time for complacency has not yet arrived. Labor relations are still capable of improvement because disputes and appeals committees are called upon to settle many cases which ought to have been resolved at local level between council officers and trade union officials.

I have the greatest regard for members of the legal profession but regret to say that, in many instances, they are responsible for the failure to reach agreement on a point of dispute with a trade union. This is because from their training and from force of habit, solicitors are apt to interpret a trade agreement as though it were an Act of Parliament or a Statutory Order.

A trade agreement is, in fact, something quite different although it may sometimes be couched in quasi-legal language. National and provincial agreements covering the pay and conditions of employees in local government are not drawn up by parliamentary draftsmen but by the joint efforts of representatives of councils and trade unions, and it would be fortuitous if a single solicitor were to be found among them.

To the professional lawyer this may seem imprudent. Nevertheless the people on both sides of the table know the meaning and intention of the agreement which has been reached and which they have expressed in their own form of words.

Sitting for many years as a member of provincial disputes committees, I have listened to solicitors stating cases on behalf of their councils and in many cases it quickly became apparent that their arguments were based solely on their interpretation of the words of the agreement, to the exclusion of the *intention* behind the words.

Clerks of councils are clearly taken aback to find they have lost cases which appeared to them to be "cast-iron" and I suppose that, to a solicitor, the taking into account of the intention of the agreement must seem like hitting below the belt.

When the wording of a national agreement is the subject of a dispute at provincial level, it is not unusual for the provincial disputes committee deliberately to fail to reach agreement so that the case may stand referred to the national disputes committee whose members know the intention of the national council which made the agreement.

The lesson to be learned from this is that an officer experienced in the application of agreements would either have reached a settlement with the trade union or, if he judged the case to be worth taking before the disputes committee, would in most instances prove a better advocate than a solicitor.

Most of the larger local authorities employ an establishment [staff] officer who should be responsible for conducting negotiations with trade unions and who should represent the council before a disputes committee. Smaller authorities which are without an establishment officer would do well to seek the advice of the employers' secretary of their provincial council before placing themselves in a position from which it would be difficult to retreat.

Most employers' secretaries possess a wealth of specialized knowledge and experience which is at the disposal of local authorities for the asking. In the event of a second opinion being thought desirable, the national employers' secretary and his staff are always willing to help. . . .

Nothing is calculated to cause trouble more quickly than the issue of instructions without giving to the people concerned the reasons why changes are necessary. Once a trade union official is satisfied that the interests of his members will not be adversely affected by proposed changes his cooperation can provide valuable help in achieving a smooth changeover to a new system.

There is no reason why a small authority, having no establishment officer, should not adopt a similar course. It would not be a waste of time for the clerk of the council, or a senior member of his staff, to hold regular meetings of this sort, thereby resolving many minor difficulties and preventing serious disputes.

Some councils rely for good staff relationships on joint committees for various groups of staff. Such committees are often set up at the request of the trade unions and in some cases do valuable work. In many instances, however, joint committees languish from lack of interest after the novelty has worn off, or become a platform used by a few militant trouble-makers to further their own ends.

In local government it is the transport department which seems to be most vulnerable to strikes, followed at a considerable distance by the public cleansing department.

Introduction of the summer or winter schedule is a frequent cause of trouble because no schedule, however carefully devised, is likely to satisfy every one of hundreds of employees. . . .

I suggest that most of these difficulties could be resolved before reaching an acute stage if adequate consultation took place in an atmosphere of mutual confidence engendered by a history of good relationships and ample communications right down the line.

Local authorities which are bedeviled by labor troubles would be well advised to review carefully their present procedures.

It is the man on the ground floor who must ultimately be convinced that he is getting a square deal—this may, and often does, involve a great deal of time and infinite patience, but there is no short cut to success if good labor relations are to be achieved and preserved.

VII. WHAT'S AHEAD

EDITOR'S INTRODUCTION

Over the years, the concepts of a professional civil service and systems of appointment and promotion by merit have been advocated as an alternative to the political spoils system. Eugene F. Berrodin, in the first selection, examines the effect collective bargaining may have on these concepts. In the final two selections, Frank P. Zeidler and Jean J. Couturier, both with broad nonpartisan background in public administration, look ahead to the next decade and consider possible developments in collective bargaining for public employees. Solutions must be found, as Mr. Couturier intimates, in line with the public good; consequently, the ordinary citizen's interest in public sector bargaining becomes more and more important.

THE FUTURE OF MERIT SYSTEMS [1]

Some observers believe collective bargaining will result in greater participation by employees in the decision-making process of government. They foresee a kind of industrial democracy in the public employment relationship. While greater participation by employee organizations in the employment relationship will occur, it is by no means certain that institutionalized bargaining will not result in a new formalism with its rigidities and vested interests. The events of the next decade will disclose more clearly the results of the changes in public personnel systems caused by public employee bargaining.

Until the post World War II period, public employee unions had been staunch supporters of civil service sys-

[1] From "By Merit or by Union," by Eugene F. Berrodin, manager, personnel and services division, Michigan Municipal League. *National Civic Review*. 57:556-60+. D. '68. Reprinted by permission.

tems. For example, the constitution of the American Federation of State, County and Municipal Employees stated that one of its objectives was "to promote civil service legislation and career service in government."

While many public employee union locals, and particularly independent employee associations, continue to advocate and support civil service systems, AFSCME has substantially withdrawn its support in favor of the industrial style of collective bargaining. . . .

The traditional view of more or less autonomous civil service commissions is that they are neutrals, representing employees, management and the public. Where a civil service agency does not wish to or cannot assume the role of representing management, collective bargaining activities may be performed by a separate office. . . .

To some extent, the development of merit systems for public employees paralleled the growth of industrial labor unions. These merit systems are quite common in the United States in the Federal service, in most states and in the larger cities. However, the application of merit principles varies widely as to coverage and adequacy.

The term *civil service* is reported to have originated in the British administration of India. It was brought into England in the 1850s where the term was applied to domestic branches of the government. In the more modern sense, civil service has a variety of meanings, depending upon the context in which it is used. *Civil service system* generally refers to a mechanism of public employment in which the selection and retention of employees is required by law to be based upon merit and fitness as determined by a competitive (examination) process.

In recent years there has been conflict between those who advocate a strong central civil service system and those who urge a more "flexible" merit system. The International City Managers' Association in its text on *Municipal Personnel Administration* favors the merit system approach with the personnel function integrated with the general powers of the city manager. The city manager appoints the personnel director or, in the smaller cities, serves as personnel director. There is continuing controversy as to the viability of semi-autonomous civil service systems in the environment of modern urban pressures. Some critics contend that the battle for merit in public employment has been won and that the semiautonomous civil service systems have outlived their usefulness. They also contend that the traditional systems reward mediocrity at the expense of superior performance.

Civil service defenders point to traditional systems which have been relatively successful, effective and corruption free. Such systems are found in Detroit, Philadelphia, Los Angeles and Denver, to mention only a few of the larger and better known civil service systems. Any administrative system is dependent for reasonable success upon adequate financial support. In some instances the failure of legislatures and executives to provide civil service agencies with even minimal financing and manpower has resulted in a failure of the system to reach its stated goals (an effective work force).

The International City Managers' Association distinguishes between civil service and merit system on the basis that civil service is a restrictive, more rigid concept structured around a semiautonomous commission or board. It refers to merit system as a more inclusive and preferable term applied to a broad goal of public personnel transactions based upon merit. The distinction lies in civil service requiring legal authorization, a semiautonomous board or commission and a formal system of administration.

It has been quite accurately observed that civil service reform was motivated by merit principles, but some civil service systems have been perverted to partisan advantage or to rigid mechanisms for assuring tenure of employees and excluding outsiders from promotional competition. Some systems have also been unresponsive to the demands for change aimed at increasing efficiency. In general, civil service and merit systems continue to have considerable popular support, particularly in the larger jurisdictions. There have been no recent proposals for the abandonment of the Federal civil service system nor for the elimination of various state systems. . . .

In determining the degree of civil service or merit system independence, the following factors are significant:

1. Method of appointment of personnel officer (by civil service board, chief executive, with or without confirmation)
2. Is the personnel officer included in the career service?
3. Method of appointment (and removal) of civil service board
4. Powers of civil service board
   a. recruitment and examining
   b. position classification
   c. compensation
   d. rule making
   e. review of disciplinary and other personnel actions
   f. employee training and safety
   g. employee relations

Clearly, some civil service systems are much more independent than others. But even the highly independent systems are dependent upon the legislative body for some program and budgetary authorizations and all are influenced by their constituency and environment.

The variety which has been described in public personnel practices is consistent with American traditions of diversity and pluralism. Local governments have been, and are, innovators in the continuing search for effective administrative mechanisms and policies.

The American approach of variety is well suited to a dynamic society. Although future trends may be somewhat obscure, it seems likely that the more rigid and autocratic systems will be rejected in favor of relatively adaptable, inclusive and employee-involved personnel systems. Yet to be discerned is the net effect of the recent movement toward formalized collective bargaining by public employees. Professor Felix A. Nigro has said:

Recently a labor relations specialist told me that civil service was "cold turkey," meaning that it had not lived up to the justifiable expectations of the employees. Certainly there is much truth to this, but the answer is to improve the merit system and not throw out the merit principle.

UNRESOLVED ISSUES [2]

It takes a degree of rashness to look at the present realities and make judgments about the future [of collective bargaining in the public sector] but here are some likely possibilities:

Compulsory arbitration seems increasingly to be accepted as the means of settling strikes in critical functions of government. Local officials have found themselves unable to prevent strikes, whatever the laws may be, and legal penalties do not always inhibit strikers, either, so the answer now seems to be compulsory arbitration. This means that the ultimate sovereign power of government rests with the arbitrator, and arbitrators will begin to introduce a kind of common law shaping the manner of controlling management-employee relations.

Official labor boards may come into greater control of governments through their regulation of employee relations, because labor boards will bring about more fair labor practices and regulations setting forth government procedures in dealing with employees.

Civil service agencies will become an arm of management, functioning as personnel agencies and assuming the instruction of middle management and first-line supervisors on how

[2] From "Public Servants as Organized Labor," by Frank P. Zeidler, umpire for American Federation of State, County and Municipal Employees District 48 and Milwaukee County, public administration consultant, and former mayor of Milwaukee. *Personnel*. 46:51-4. Jl.-Ag. '69. Reprinted by permission of the publisher from *Personnel*, July/August 1969, © by the American Management Association, Inc.

to administer an agreement. The functions of civil service as an employee protection agency will be transferred to employee organizations.

A trend may develop for local governments to contract out work to escape problems inherent in dealing with a work force of government employees.)

The number of decision areas that have been considered prerogatives of public management will undoubtedly be reduced; management will be able to retain only what it can hold on to at the bargaining table. Similarly, past experience suggests that there will be more legislation recognizing and granting rights to employee organizations, which in turn will mean yielding of powers by the legislative bodies themselves.

The agency shop [requiring a "service fee" from employees in a collective bargaining unit who do not join the union] may appear eventually and may receive legislative sanction.

The role of the civic group as an important influence in the bargaining process is not likely to be an important factor in bargaining in the near future, but the clamor of civic groups for some voice will increase.

Legislative efforts to deal with the strike may introduce further steps in the negotiating process, in the hope that prolonging that process will lead to a solution short of a strike.

One of the most interesting developments could be Federal control over the standards and practices of employee relationships in state and local government through Federal legislation and court interpretation of clauses such as the "commerce clause" of the Constitution. Thus, Federal standards may ultimately shape state and local government employee relations.

Some major issues have not yet been resolved and are not likely to be resolved soon:

The most important of these issues is the prevention of strikes by government employees. At the moment the only control seems to be the judgment of the employees themselves, and they will not consider bargaining as fully collective until they have the legal right to strike.

Another unresolved problem is that of management's learning to cope with a very large number of employee organizations to allow ample time for negotiating. This is already almost unmanageable for some jurisdictions, and no legislative formula is in the offing for controlling the formation and recognition of bargaining units so that their number does not get completely out of hand, as far as management is concerned.

The question of who shall be designated to negotiate for state or Federal governments is wide open. Shall individual units in various places negotiate with employees in that locality? Shall there be one statewide or nationwide bargainer? The state and national aspects are far more complicated than those at the local level. A related problem is whether there should be statewide or regional bargaining for all employees in one category of work. Areawide bargaining may finally emerge, and, anticipating this contingency, local governments had better study this problem now.

The theoretical discussion of the differences between employment in the public services and private industry will continue, especially of the public employees' argument that there is no difference and they therefore should have the right to strike.

A very basic question concerns the right of the individual employee not to join an employee organization but still be heard in the process of wage setting when there is exclusive union representation. Of all the questions on public employee relations, this is by far the most difficult about which to arrive at a formula, and perhaps that is why it is ignored in practice.

Fitting the budgeting process to collective negotiation so that statutory deadlines are met poses special difficulties to which there is as yet no solution. Perhaps administrators must reconcile themselves to the fact that some part of their budget will always have an open end, that negotiations simply will not be packaged within statutory requirements for budgets.

Local and state governments are finding it hard to protect their legislative fronts, because some employee organizations that cannot win all their demands through bargaining are successful in getting legislation that compels local government to yield what it did not give up in negotiations. This flank attack is often deplored by public administrators and union leaders alike, but they might as well recognize that the practice will continue. . . .

The Public Point of View

The implications of the new trends and developments in the public service trouble many people, for various reasons. Some think that the adversary relationship between administration and employee organization represents not only a legally structured antagonism between public administration and employees, but also an encroachment of employees on government, portending the ultimate control of government by employee organizations.

A more positive view is that formal organization of employees is, first, inevitable because of the increasingly large number of employees in the public service, and second, desirable because it is the only way, despite defects, for a government to maintain a satisfied and productive work force. It can be said, too, that employee organization gives an alert and progressive management excellent feedback on the impact of its policies and their effect on the morale and attitudes of employees. Some public administrators also believe that tight agreements with employees compel management to function more efficiently, that management may be improved by being forced to defend its right to manage.

A nation such as ours, expanding in population and in expectations of more services but with no increase in willingness to pay, must have exceedingly capable governmental administration at all levels. The organization and administration of a work force to meet national goals and objectives is a major function of government; if it fails, government fails.

Employee organizations under legislation that permits a voice in policy but not the controlling voice over elected legislative bodies can help meet national goals. However, effective public administration is also required to administer employee agreements, so a failure of public administrators to become competent in the field of employee relations is a disservice not only to employees but to the public. Public administrators and public employees alike should serve the people, and in their dickerings and even battles with each other, efficient functioning of vital services should not be lost sight of as the overriding interest.

CRISIS, CONFLICT, AND CHANGE [3]

The very real issues raised by the clear trend of transposing the practices of private employee unions to the government sphere are, in fact, crucial concerns for government, for the employees affected, and for the public whose services and programs are at stake. While the parties to this conflict are in process of creating a new environment, it is imperative that the citizen's voice be heard in giving direction to that change.

It is not enough to give policy guidance. There remains a critical need for further objective research; in-depth communication among those who deal with the issues on a day-to-day basis and those scholars closely concerned with government, economics, labor relations; and widespread involvement of interested citizens through all the devices of conferences, education, and information dissemination.

A look at the impact collective bargaining is likely to have on government if the current haphazard, nondirected course continues will underline these needs.

[3] From "Crisis, Conflict and Change: the Future of Collective Bargaining in Public Service," by Jean J. Couturier, executive director, National Civil Service League. *Good Government.* 86:7-11. Spring '69. Reprinted by permission.

The following are personal predictions, based on my training, observations and experiences in the fields of labor relations and public administration over twenty years. . . .

American labor relations history has been summed up as movement from conflict to accommodation to cooperation. The public sector is unique in that its early history was one of cooperation between relatively weak but large employee associations and essentially paternalistic government managements. . . .

The simple days are gone in government. Government personnel management is no longer the leader of industry. Militant unions—not reluctant to strike—challenge the traditional employee associations. Public employees are confused and disillusioned with working under complex laws and codes. Public pay, tenure, fringes are no longer ahead of industry. In fact, in many areas, the total package lags by wide margins. Tax bases erode, politicians run scared, and citizens clamor for reform.

Given these facts, it is highly likely that the number of strikes against government will continue to increase. Their length, scope, and impact will grow rapidly. Competition between independent employee associations and traditional affiliated unions will increase, and with it, demands will escalate. This trend is likely to accelerate until most public employees are organized in secure, potent organizations. Employees will deal with nonpaternalistic managements that are either hard or soft bargainers, depending on the power relationships and the relative security of the managements as *political* institutions. We will, then, not see a movement from conflict to accommodation until the smoke has cleared; until the two sides to bargaining have clarified their roles and status and have tested each other.

In this process, it is quite likely that public unionization will extend far beyond the traditional blue-collar memberships that characterize private industry unions. Though the bulk of organized public employees are nonprofessionals, a great many technicians, scientists and administrative personnel are already members of public employee groups. This mix has profound implications for both the substance of bargaining and for the nature of the institutions that will bargain.

The impact of bargaining on the substantive issues of wages and conditions of employment is already becoming clear. Here are some of the changes I see arising from the current era of crisis and conflict.

Wages of public employees will continue to rise rapidly. This rise will be greater than the national average for several years. It will be because of the lag in public employee wages, because competing organizations will escalate their demands to justify their support and achieve growth, because managements will seek to buy peace and because—in the short run—public employee organizations will become better lobbying groups and have stronger political muscle. Premium pay for overtime and holidays, now rare in government, will become nearly universal.

This upward wage pressure will take place in an environment of fear and frustration among elected chief executives and legislative bodies. The fear of seeking more taxes, the frustration of limited revenue sources will squeeze harder on officials as they try to reconcile rising public demands for services, hostility to more taxes, and ability of employees to extract higher wages. . . .

Looking at the internals of wage matters, there will be further startling changes. Civil service salary classification will continue. It will, though, have less relevance as power relationships alter the relative value placed on different classes of work and as job structures change in response to organizational demands. The already increasing trend toward community-based prevailing wage concepts—rather than statewide national uniformity—will take on added importance. Existing relationships of salary grades will be further blurred. Salary ranges will be further compressed, and movement within grades will take place in fewer steps

over shorter periods. Ultimately, executive and senior civil
service salaries will be removed from the general salary grad-
ing systems in order to get around problems of compression.
Fringe benefit patterns developed over the last ninety years
will undergo radical readjustment. Pensions will be more
and more tied to the social security system and will be transferable. They will begin to be bilaterally administered by
governments and employee organizations. Health and welfare packages will move from the legislative, civil service administered arena to negotiated bases and they too will become more and more bilaterally controlled. Employees will
win more paid time for vacations, sick leave and personal
time. And it is likely that this time will be combined in a
single leave package for all purposes that will be fully cumu-
lative and payable in full on separation.

Staffing systems in government will bear a good deal of re-
semblance to today's merit principles of hiring, assignment,
promotion and tenure based on nonpolitical factors of competence. But the methods by which these will be expressed
will differ. It is unlikely that the public service will see the
closed shop but it will see the union shop or the agency shop
in which all must pay for organizational services. Hence,
these will become a new element in determining tenure.

Management Will Hire

Hiring practices will remain with management, but with
increasing pressure for employee participation in developing
examinations. Lateral entry of qualified people outside government at higher levels will continue to be discouraged, if
only because many personnel people share employees' false
view that this protection of the insider against the outsider
is part of the merit principle. . . . But this too will change.
In part, it will be because of factors other than labor relations—skill shortages, pressures from the disadvantaged, increasing employee mobility, for example. Line management
will react to strong labor contracts by slowly winning freedom to bring outsiders in at higher echelons.

Promotion systems won't change much. Most civil services have built-in seniority provisions already. Though these are likely to be strengthened, they will not reach the pervasive force they represent in private industry. This, in part, is because most civil servants remain wedded to a belief that the examination system is less arbitrary and generally fairer than promotions based on tenure alone or on other factors. Promotional system continuity, combined with opposition to lateral entry, is likely to keep civil service an essentially closed system for many years, or until other pressures force change.

Together, these will bring added burdens to citizens and to governments as they seek to modernize government, make it more responsive and react effectively to the creation of public service job opportunities for many who are now frozen out. Two results are likely to be: more use of contractor-supplied personnel and government hiring outside the civil service systems. In the latter, I think here of concepts such as the "employer of last resort" and more pressures to differentiate between government workers and civil servants.

Grievance resolution will probably revolutionize the management of government. Employee organizations will become deeply involved in changing the day-to-day working environment through development of sophisticated grievance machinery. The machinery will increasingly be tripartite, and binding arbitration of grievances will become common.

Adverse action, or disciplinary, procedures will change radically. Today's complex systems of charges, hearings, transcripts, appeals and court proceedings will slowly give way to typical industrial arbitration, with neutrals controlling the outcome. At first, arbitration will be fairly informal, but as precedents are established and a body of equity law is built through arbitration, the process will become more formalized. It will then begin to reach the complexity of today's disciplinary procedures. Arbitration will directly affect the rule-making role of civil service bodies, ultimately challenging much of the traditional civil service commission's authority.

Program missions of governmental agencies will increasingly become subjects of collective bargaining. Private industry is profit motivated. Public industry is service motivated. While both are also motivated by the will to perpetuate those in power, the means of so doing are radically different. Most corporations are essentially self-governing and self-perpetuating in terms of directorships and executive leadership. Government officials are totally dependent on the political process in its broadest context. Hence, the mission of the private organization—to produce goods or services for profit and continuity—is largely in the hands of management if the management doesn't make too many major mistakes. But the mission of government agencies is subjected to the will of the people and to the whole spectrum of political considerations.

Unions and Program Mission

These differences, among others, have generally meant that private industry unions have tried to avoid involvement in industry mission. Unions don't want the responsibility of deciding how many cars, what color, at what price, etc., will be produced.

This is not the case in public service bargaining. Teachers' unions want—and strike to win—a voice on whom they will teach, and under what circumstances. Welfare workers bargain over services to give. Air traffic controllers become deeply involved in the very heart of airport safety measures. Presumably, it is the citizens who, through their legislatures, have determined the scope, quality, and nature of services government will provide. When we consider the potential economic, job control, and political powers of public employee organizations, we know we are faced with extremely delicate, critical questions as to the direction of our society. We face, too, the question of *who* will decide this direction.

All these factors will have a far-reaching impact on government personnel management and on the systems of public administration. . . .

The three most critical areas of institutional change concern the chief executive and legislative bodies, the merit principle and civil service systems of personnel management, and the employee organizations. Collective bargaining augurs great changes in all these institutions, changes with implications for the very roots of our system of government.

Chief executives and legislatures will have to adjust their roles radically. Public employee payrolls account for about one third of all state-local government expenditures. Budgetary processes are long and involved. Collective bargaining may very well prohibit the leisure of spending from six months to a year and a half in building and getting approval of budgets that include personnel services. Thus, wage settlements, cost items resulting from grievance resolutions, and the budgetary impact of continuous bargaining will further the national trend of centering authority in the chief elected executive.

The chief executive will get authority to commit public funds quickly without going through the long legislative process. As is already happening in some states and localities and is beginning to happen in the Federal arena, the chief executive will be able to set wages. His monetary commitment will be either subject only to legislative veto or will become a "mandatory item" in budgets submitted to legislatures. . . .

If binding arbitration of contract disputes—such as has . . . been legislated in Pennsylvania for some jurisdictions —becomes widespread, the fiscal roles of both the legislatures and the chief executive will be greatly diminished. Whether this practice will take deep roots depends on many factors. Governments and employee organizations are, in general, opposed. But it is quite possible that the public will demand it. The probable grounds for such demands will be opposition to strikes that disrupt services, or revulsion against real or imagined collusion between elected officials and employee representatives in which public money is traded for political support.

Merit principles and civil service systems will be profoundly affected. The merit principle of employment, assignment, promotion and tenure is likely to remain part of our better governments. But where it is not now deeply rooted, it will be more difficult to achieve. The likely development here is that the political patronage machines of politicians will be weakened by the rise of a new form of patronage—that of the employee organization which will be politically powerful and will work to achieve more direct control of jobs, promotions and discharge.

Employee organizations of tomorrow will be much different from those of today. They will be more militant. They will be more professional. The necessity to provide services in depth, particularly in grievance handling, but also in contract negotiation, will mean that they will have to be more firmly financed. The advent of exclusive recognition will slowly do away with splinter organizations and multiple representation, thus forcing the exclusive representative to be more responsible and responsive to its membership.

As managements move from paternalism—benevolent or otherwise—so, too, will employee organizations shift from being supplicants to being bargainers. This, and the necessity to compete for rank-and-file employee loyalty, will make many employee organizations rethink policies of all-inclusive membership. Management will successfully raise conflict-of-interest arguments that will further force organizations to exclude supervisors from their memberships.

Competition between unions affiliated with the AFL-CIO and independent associations will, in the short run, sharpen. Each will assume much of the philosophy of the other. For instance, as affiliated unions win exclusive recognition, they will move from the highly militant organizing stages to still militant, but secure, more cautious institutions. Conversely, unaffiliated associations will at first become more militant. And, as the two kinds of organizations become more alike than different, other changes will take place. Independent associations will be forced to raise dues substantially, both to compete in the short run and to provide in-depth services to members in the long run.

This, then, is the picture of crisis, conflict and change I see in the future of collective bargaining in the public service. We are in for several years of great crisis. Conflict between employees and governments, between employees and the public they serve, and between employee organizations will continue beyond the crisis stage. This will continue until change salves the wounds. Then a period of accommodation will ensue. Whether we will in ten years see collective bargaining in the public service characterized by a climate of cooperation will depend on the wisdom of the parties, and, in the final analysis, on the ability of the citizen to guide and cope with the issues.

BIBLIOGRAPHY

An asterisk (*) preceding a reference indicates that the article or a part of it has been reprinted in this book.

BOOKS, PAMPHLETS, AND DOCUMENTS

*American Assembly. Challenges to collective bargaining [papers prepared under the editorial supervision of Dr. Lloyd Ulman for the thirtieth American Assembly, October 1966]. Prentice-Hall. '67.
> Reprinted in this book: Collective bargaining in the public sector. Jack Stieber. p 69-73.

Anderson, H. J. ed. Public employee organization and bargaining; a report on the joint conference of the Association of Labor Mediation Agencies and the National Association of State Labor Relations Agencies, August 19 to 24, 1968. Bureau of National Affairs, Inc. 1231 24th St. N.W. Washington, D.C. 20037. '68.

Benjamin, H. C. Collective bargaining and the hospitals. (Selected References no 145) Industrial Relations Section. Princeton University. Princeton, N.J. 08540. '69.

Bieson, Chester. The ABC's of collective bargaining. (Information Bulletin no 306) Association of Washington Cities. 3935 University Way, N.E. Seattle 98105. '68.

*Christensen, T. G. S. ed. Proceedings of New York University twenty-first annual conference on labor. Bender. '69.
> Reprinted in this book: Public employees and collective bargaining: comparative and local experience. Arvid Anderson. p 451-69; How to prevent strikes by public employees. T. W. Kheel. p 566-75.

Colorado Legislative Council. Public employee negotiations, report to the Colorado General Assembly. (Research Publication no 142) mimeo. The Council. Room 341, State Capitol. Denver 80203. '68.

Doherty, R. E. and Oberer, W. E. Teachers, school boards, and collective bargaining: a changing of the guard. (ILR paperback no 2) New York State School of Industrial and Labor Relations. Cornell University. Ithaca, N.Y. 14850. '67.

Doherty, R. E. and others, eds. The changing employment relationship in public schools. New York State School of Industrial and Labor Relations. Cornell University. Ithaca, N.Y. 14850. '66.

Dunlop, J. T. and Chamberlain, N. W. eds. Frontiers of collective bargaining. Harper. '67.

Elam, S. M. and others. Readings on collective negotiations in public education. Rand McNally. '67.

Godine, M. R. The labor problem in the public service; a study in political pluralism. Russell and Russell. '67.

Haak, H. H. Collective bargaining and academic governance: the case of the California state colleges. Public Affairs Research Institute. San Diego State College. San Diego, Calif. 92115. '68.

Hanslowe, K. L. The emerging law of labor relations in public employment. (ILR paperback no 4) New York State School of Industrial and Labor Relations. Cornell University. Ithaca, N.Y. 14850. '67.

Heisel, W. D. and Hallihan, J. D. Questions & answers on public employee negotiation. Public Personnel Association. 1313 E. 60th St. Chicago 60307. '67.

Helsby, R. D. Public employment labor relations: yesterday's heresy, today's policy; address before the seventh annual institute of the American Society for Public Administration, April 2, 1969. mimeo. New York State Public Employment Relations Board. 875 Central Ave. Albany 12206. '69.

*Henley, J. W. Canadian experience; address before American Management Association personnel conference, New York City, February 4, 1969. mimeo. The author. Hamilton, Ont. '69.

*Morse, Wayne. Government view of the state of collective bargaining; address before American Management Association personnel conference, New York City, February 4, 1969. The Association. New York. '69.
    Copies of this News Release are no longer available.

New York State. Governor's Committee on Public Employee Relations. Final report, March 31, 1966. The Committee. Albany. '66.

New York State. Governor's Committee on Public Employee Relations. Interim report, June 17, 1968. The Committee. Albany. '68.

New York State. Governor's Committee on Public Employee Relations. Report of January 23, 1969. The Committee. Albany. '69.

New York State. Public Employment Relations Board. Summary of the proceedings of governor's conference on public employment relations. mimeo. The Board. 875 Central Ave. Albany 12206. '68.

*New York State. Public Employment Relations Board. Year one of
the Taylor Law, September 1, 1967-August 31, 1968. The
Board. 875 Central Ave. Albany 12206. '68.

Oberer, W. E. and others. The Taylor Act: a primer for school
personnel (and other beginners at collective negotiations).
(Bulletin no 59) New York State School of Industrial and
Labor Relations. Cornell University. Ithaca, N.Y. 14850. '67.
Prepared at the request of New York State Department of Education.

Ocheltree, Keith, ed. Perspective in public employee negotiation.
(Public Employee Relations Library. Special issue) Public
Personnel Association. 1313 E. 60th St. Chicago 60637. '69.

Ontario. Royal Commission. Report: inquiry into labour disputes;
I. C. Rand. Frank Fogg, Queen's Printer. Toronto. '68.

Organization Resources Counselors, Inc. Selected bibliography on
collective bargaining—public employees. mimeo. The Organization. 1270 Avenue of the Americas. New York 10020. '67.

Polisar, Eric. Strikes and solutions. (Public Employee Relations
Library no 7) Public Personnel Association. 1313 E. 60th St.
Chicago 60637. '68.

Roberts, H. S. Labor-management relations in the public service.
Industrial Relations Center. University of Hawaii. 2500 Campus Rd. Honolulu 96822. '68.

Rubin, R. S. Summary of state collective bargaining law in public
employment. (Public Employee Relations Reports, 3) New
York State School of Industrial and Labor Relations. Cornell
University. Ithaca, N.Y. 14850. '68.

Schlachter, Gail, ed. Collective bargaining: a selected basic bibliography. mimeo. John R. Commons Industrial Relations Reference Center. Industrial Relations Research Institute. University of Wisconsin. Madison 53706. '68.

Schmidt, C. T. Jr. and others. Guide to collective negotiations in
education. [Michigan] Research and Planning Division. School
of Labor and Industrial Relations. 402 Kedzie Hall. Michigan
State University. East Lansing 48823. '67.

Somers, G. G. ed. Collective bargaining in the public service. Industrial Relations Research Association. Social Science Building. Madison, Wis. 53706. '66.

Thompson, A. W. J. Strikes and strike penalties in public employment. (Public Employee Report no 2) New York State School
of Industrial and Labor Relations. Cornell University. Ithaca,
N.Y. 14850. '67.

Tompkins, D. C. comp. Strikes by public employees and professional personnel: a bibliography. Institute of Governmental
Studies. University of California. Berkeley 94720. '67.

Tracy, E. R. Arbitration cases in public employment. American Arbitration Association. 140 W. 51st St. New York 10020. '69.

Triplett, J. E. ed. Collective bargaining for public employees; proceedings of a conference sponsored by the Institute of Industrial and Labor Relations, the Division of Continuing Education, University of Oregon, Eugene [Nov. 18, 1966]. The Division. University of Oregon. Eugene 97403. '67.

*United States. Congress. Senate. Committee on Post Office and Civil Service. Employee-management relations in the Federal service; hearings before the Committee, on S. 341, July 11 and 12, 1968. 90th Congress, 2nd session. The Committee. Washington, D.C. '68.

> Reprinted in this book: Statement by Representative Benjamin B. Blackburn (Republican, Georgia), July 11, 1968 [excerpts].

*United States. Department of Labor. Fifty-sixth annual report, fiscal year 1968. Supt. of Docs. Washington, D.C. 20402. '69.

> Reprinted in this book: Draft report of the President's review committee on employee-management relations in the Federal service, April 1968. Attachment B. p 1-20.

United States. Department of Labor. Bureau of Labor Statistics. Directory of national and international labor unions in the United States, 1967; prepared by F. R. Nagy and others. (Bulletin no 1596) Supt. of Docs. Washington, D.C. 20402. '68.

United States. Department of Labor. Labor-Management Services Administration. Policy for employee-management cooperation in the Federal service. The Department. Washington, D.C. 20210. '61.

United States. Department of Labor. Labor-Management Services Administration. Office of Labor-Management Policy Development. Federal employee unit arbitration. The Department. Washington, D.C. 20210. '69.

> Includes: Text of Executive Order 10988.

United States. Department of Labor. Library. Employee-management relations in the public service [selected references]. (Current Bibliographies no 1) The Department. Washington, D.C. 20210. '67.

United States. President. Executive Order 10988, signed by President John F. Kennedy, January 17, 1962; employee-management cooperation in the Federal service. Supt. of Docs. Washington, D.C. 20402. '62.

University of Hawaii. Legislative Reference Bureau. Hawaii constitutional convention studies: Article XII—organization, collective bargaining. The Bureau. 2425 Campus Rd. Honolulu 96822. '68.

Warner, K. O. ed. Collective bargaining in the public service: theory and practice. Public Personnel Association. 1313 E. 60th St. Chicago 60637. '67.

Warner, K. O. ed. Management relations with organized public employees. Public Personnel Association. 1313 E. 60th St. Chicago 60637. '63.

Warner, K. O. and Hennessy, M. L. Public management at the bargaining table. Public Personnel Association. 1313 E. 60th St. Chicago 60637. '67.

PERIODICALS

AAUP (American Association of University Professors) Bulletin. 53:217-27. Je. '67. Collective bargaining issues in the California state colleges. C. M. Larsen.

*AAUP (American Association of University Professors) Bulletin. 54:155-9. Je. '68. Faculty participation in strikes.

AAUP (American Association of University Professors) Bulletin. 54:160-8. Je. '68. The strike and the professoriate. S. H. Kadish.

AAUP (American Association of University Professors) Bulletin. 54:365-8. S. '68. California state colleges: adoption of a system-wide grievance procedure. S. S. Buchalter and H. H. Haak.

ALA Bulletin. 62:973-6. S. '68. Collective bargaining—some questions asked. G. L. Gardiner.

ALA Bulletin. 62:1385-90. D. '68. Collective bargaining: questions and answers.

ALA Bulletin. 63:363-8. Mr. '69. Librarians Association at the University of California. Eldred Smith.

*ALA Bulletin. 63:455-64. Ap. '69. A new dimension in library administration—negotiating a union contract. Robert Lewis.

America. 115:455-7. O. 15, '66. Cities on strike. Michael Parks.

America. 117:609-10. N. 18, '67. Strikes against government. B. L. Masse.

America. 119:63. Ag. 3, '68. Two unions that are going places. B. L. Masse.

American City. 82:50-1. Mr. '67. How to negotiate with municipal labor unions.

American City. 83:8. Jl. '68. Collective bargaining vs. civil service. Nelson Howorth.

American Federationist. 74:15-18. Jl. '67. Public employees: an emerging force. D. L. Perlman.

American Labor. 1:21-6. Je. '68. Public employee unions.

American Labor. 2:41-5. Ap. '69. America's teachers.

American School Board Journal. 155:7-15+. O., 7-18. N. '67. Negotiations (symposium). Myron Lieberman and others.

American School Board Journal. 155:23-4. Mr. '68. "Mass sickness" doesn't pay in Camden. M. C. Nolte.

*American School Board Journal. 155:26-7. Mr. '68. Alternative to collective bargaining. R. L. Walter.

American School Board Journal. 156:9-13. N. '68. The tough new teacher.

Arbitration Journal. 21:24-33. '66. Public disputes and the public interest. J. W. Teele.

Arbitration Journal. 21:93-7. '66. Is collective bargaining the answer? comments on a municipal labor crisis. T. A. Knowlton.

Arbitration Journal. 22:31-9. '67. Rights and responsibilities in municipal collective bargaining. D. J. White.

Arbitration Journal. 22:40-7. '67. Philosophy of bargaining for municipal employees. Allan Weisenfeld.

*Arbitration Journal. 23:69-84. '68. Why public employees strike. A. M. Zack.

Arbitration Journal. 24:106-15. '69. Fact-finding: is it adjudication or adjustment? R. J. Jossen.

Atlantic Monthly. 221:46-51. Ja. '68. Strikes by public employees. A. H. Raskin.

Business Week. p 92+. D. 3, '66. Public employees ask for a better shake.

Business Week. p 98. Ap. 8, '67. Can new state law end public worker strikes?

Business Week. p 76-8. O. 21, '67. Where unions have most growth potential: unionism among public employees.

Business Week. p 122. Mr. 2, '68. Cure for public employee strikes.

Business Week. p 100. Ag. 17, '68. Teachers get militant.

Canadian Public Administration. 11:485-93. Winter '68. Some aspects of policy determination in the development of the collective bargaining legislation in the public service of Canada. Robert Armstrong.

De Paul Law Review. 16:151-65. Autumn-Winter '66. Right of public employees to strike. Herbert Hoffman.

Drake Law Review. 18:26-46. D. '68. Collective bargaining in the public sector: a survey of major options. V. L. Schoenthal.

Dun's Review. 91:51-2+. Je. '68. Public employees: they're going to strike. Murray Seeger.

Fortune. 78:104-7+. Ag. '68. Those newly militant government workers. Irwin Ross.

*Good Government. 85:9-15. Spring '68. Strikes in public employment. G. W. Taylor.

Good Government. 85:15-20. Spring '68. Civil servants and the strike. Jerome Lefkowitz.
   Same. Michigan Municipal Review. 41:226+. S. '68.

Good Government. 85:11-15. Fall '68. Implications of collective bargaining for public personnel management. D. E. Streiff.

Good Government. 86:3-6. Spring '69. What every civil service commissioner needs to know about labor relations. F. A. Nigro.

*Good Government. 86:7-11. Spring '69. Crisis, conflict, and change: the future of collective bargaining in public service. J. J. Couturier.

*Good Housekeeping. 168:12+. Ap. '69. The GH poll: Should teachers have the right to strike?

Government Employee Relations Report
       Weekly with cumulative index. Published by Bureau of National Affairs. 1231 25th St. N.W. Washington, D. C. 20037.

Industrial and Labor Relations Review. 19:573-95. Jl. '66. Determination of bargaining units and election procedures in public school teacher representation elections. R. E. Doherty.

Industrial and Labor Relations Review. 20:3-29. O. '66. Wisconsin public employee factfinding procedure. J. L. Stern.

Industrial and Labor Relations Review. 20:179-97. Ja. '67. Role of state agencies in public employee labor relations. J. T. McKelvey.

Industrial and Labor Relations Review. 20:457-77. Ap. '67. Cook county (Ill.) commissioners' factfinding board report on collective bargaining and county public aid employees. J. T. McKelvey.

Industrial and Labor Relations Review. 20:617-36. Jl. '67. Public employment: strikes or procedures? G. W. Taylor.

Industrial and Labor Relations Review. 21:541-58. Jl. '68. Labor-management policy for public employees in Illinois: the experience of the governor's commission, 1966-1967. Milton Derber.

*Industrial and Labor Relations Review. 22:20-30. O. '68. TVA looks at three decades of collective bargaining. A. J. Wagner.

Industrial and Labor Relations Review. 22:528-43. Jl. '69. Factfinding in public employment disputes: promise or illusion? J. T. McKelvey.

Industrial Relations. 5:86-104. My. '66. Labor relations in New York City. A. H. Cook and L. S. Gray.

Industrial Relations. 7:80-91. O. '67. The ILO and Japanese public employee unions. Morrison Handsaker and Marjorie Handsaker.

Industrial Relations. 7:93-106. F. '68. Professional negotiations in education. J. W. Garbarino.

International Labour Review. 95:239-41. Mr. '67. Trade union rights of public employees in Japan.

Labor Law Journal. 17:532-40. S. '66. Public employment fact-finding in fourteen states; survey of current legislation. E. B. Krinsky.

Labor Law Journal. 18:90-102. F. '67. Qualified right to strike; in the public interest. J. H. Foegen.

*Labor Law Journal. 18:236-45. Ap. '67. Nurses, collective bargaining and labor legislation. Archie Kleingartner.

Labor Law Journal. 18:323-35. Je. '67. New York Taylor law: a preliminary assessment. W. B. Gould.

Labor Law Journal. 18:406-11. Jl. '67. Pitfalls of collective bargaining in public employment. J. R. Clary.

Labor Law Journal. 18:412-19. Jl. '67. Collective bargaining in education: the anatomy of a problem. W. R. Hazard.

*Labor Law Journal. 18:727-38. D. '67. AFGE and the AFSCME: labor's hope for the future? H. A. Donoian.

Labor Law Journal. 18:752-5. D. '67. Compatibility of public employment collective bargaining with public interests. J. N. Ray.

Labor Law Journal. 19:273-82. My. '68. Striking teachers, welfare, transit and sanitation workers. P. J. Montana.

Labor Law Journal. 19:283-91. My. '68. Question of the recognition of principal and other supervisory units in public education collective bargaining. C. T. Schmidt, Jr.

Labor Law Journal. 19:387-90. Jl. '68. A new frontier in collective bargaining; address. Sam Zagoria.

Labor Law Journal. 19:569-89. S. '68. Bargaining in the Federal sector. C. B. Craver.

Labor Law Journal. 19:615-27. O. '68. Strike as a professional sanction: the changing attitude of the National Education Association. J. D. Muir.

Labor Law Journal. 19:681-6. N. '68. Impact of automation on labor-management relations in government. Husain Mustafa.

Labor Law Journal. 19:778-804. D. '68. Collective bargaining in universities and colleges. T. H. Ferguson.

Labor Law Journal. 20:264-88. My. '69. New York public employee relations laws. H. H. Rains.

Labor Law Journal. 20:438-44. Jl. '69. First Amendment right of association for public employee union members. J. M. Eisner.

*Labor Today. 7:24-8. Fall '68. Unionism in higher education. P. A. Grant, Jr.

Labor Today. 8:30-3. My. '69. New York city teachers' strikes. Richard Parrish.

Labour Gazette (Canada. Department of Labour). 67:626. O. '67. Collective bargaining in the public service. W. R. Cunningham.

Labour Gazette (Canada. Department of Labour). 68:318-25. Je.
'68. Emerging sectors of collective bargaining [McGill industrial relations conference].

Labour Gazette (Canada. Department of Labour). 68:391. Jl. '68.
First public service collective agreements.

Library Journal. 92:2115-21. Je. 1, '67. Libraries and labor unions.
K. Nyren.

Library Journal. 93:717-20. F. 15, '68. Librarians and unions: the
Berkeley experience. Eldred Smith.

*Library Journal. 93:4105-6. N. 1, '68. Unionization is not inevitable. K. M. Cottam.

Library Journal. 93:4107-12. N. 1, '68. Report from the picket line.
Lois Huish and others.

Library Journal. 94:475-6. F. 1, '69. Go-slow strike: letter to the
editor. Jeremiah Post.

Library Journal. 94:3403-7. O. 1, '69. Unions in libraries. J. S.
Hopkins.

Life. 64:4. Mr. 1, '68. Strikes that can't be tolerated.

Look. 32:64-6+. S. 3, '68. Our angry teachers. Jack Star.

*MSU (Michigan State University) Business Topics. 15:67-71. Autumn '67. New approach to strikes in public employment.
Jack Stieber.

Management of Personnel Quarterly. 7:20-3. Fall '68. Teacher
strikes: their causes and their impact. Kenneth McLennan and
M. H. Moskow.

*Michigan Municipal Review. 41:227+. S. '68. Compulsory arbitration: a Pandora's box. H. G. Marsh.

Midstream. 13:36-47. D. '67. The New York teachers' strike. Deborah Meier.

Minnesota Municipalities. 52:130-2+. My. '67. New dimension in
labor-management partnership. L. J. Kroeger.

Missouri Law Review. 33:409-25. Summer '68. Subjects of collective
bargaining in the public service: not really collective bargaining. D. P. Sullivan.

Monthly Labor Review. 89:603-23. Je. '66. Collective bargaining in
the public sector [special issue].

Monthly Labor Review. 89:728-32. Jl. '66. Representation among
teachers. M. H. Moskow.

Monthly Labor Review. 90:43-6. Ag. '67. Work stoppages and
teachers: history and prospect. R. W. Glass.

Monthly Labor Review. 90:22-5. S. '67. Reflections on professional
organization; excerpt from address. P. C. Briant.

Monthly Labor Review. 90:19-20. N. '67. AFT in caucus and convention: new style for 1967. B. S. Julian.

*Monthly Labor Review. 91:36-40. My. '68. Labor relations for policemen and firefighters; excerpt from address, February 29, 1968. J. J. Loewenberg.
*Monthly Labor Review. 91:48-55. Je. '68. Labor-management relations laws in public service. J. P. Goldberg.
Monthly Labor Review. 91:27-36. Jl. '68. Representation of classroom teachers: two case studies, Detroit and Grand Rapids. C. T. Schmidt, Jr.
Monthly Labor Review. 91:53. Jl. '68. Work stoppages in government. J. T. Hall, Jr.
Monthly Labor Review. 91:18-20. N. '68. AFT: local control, money and merger. A. M. Ross.
Monthly Labor Review. 91:37-9. D. '68. Bargaining units in the Federal service. H. J. Lahne.
Monthly Labor Review. 92:31-4. Ja. '69. Prospects for white-collar unionism; excerpt from address, September 1968. H. M. Douty.
*Monthly Labor Review. 92:41-6. Ja. '69. Review of state labor laws enacted in 1968. C. T. Sorenson.
*Monthly Labor Review. 92:14-18. Mr. '69. Public employee unions and the right to strike. A. M. Ross.
*Monthly Labor Review. 92:47-9. Mr. '69. Public employee bargaining in Europe [excerpt from paper presented at meeting of Industrial Relations Research Association, December 29-30, 1968]. E. M. Kassalow.
Monthly Labor Review. 92:27-9. My. '69. FMCS and dispute mediation in the Federal Government. Willoughby Abner.
Monthly Labor Review. 92:60-9. Jl. '69. Collective bargaining in the public sector; excerpts from addresses at collective bargaining forum. D. L. Cole and others.
*Municipal and Public Services Journal (London). 76:309+. F. 9, '68. Labour relations in local government. W. A. Pullan.
NEA Journal. 55:18-20. Ap. '66. Unionism versus professionalism in teaching. R. D. Batchelder.
NEA Journal. 55:54. My. '66. Teacher-opinion poll: should teachers strike?
National Civic Review. 55:332-3. Je. '66. Massachusetts passes law on public bargaining. C. D. Saso.
National Civic Review. 56:392-7. Jl. '67. At the bargaining table: state laws, Federal standards differ greatly, on rights of public employee unions and duties of the employers. E. F. Berrodin.
*National Civic Review. 57:556-60+. D. '68. By merit or by union. E. F. Berrodin.
Nation's Business. 55:38-42. N. '67. More costly strikes ahead: rising strength of public employee unions.

New Republic. 156:10-11. F. 25, '67. Unionizing the academics. James Brann.

New York Post. p 3. D. 17, '68. Short history of 1968, year of the strike. Timothy Lee.

New York State Bar Journal. 40:86-93. F. '68. Condon-Wadlin act: a study in legislative futility. J. J. Pauletti and S. R. Worth.

New York Times. p 49. N. 29, '68. Two very different trials (hospital and teachers' strikes) . S. E. Zion.

New York Times. p 29. F. 16, '69. Arbiters urged in U.S. disputes. Damon Stetson.

New York Times. p 23. Ap. 8, '69. N. E. A. urges law to guarantee negotiation in teacher disputes. E. C. Burks.

New York Times. p 49. Je. 8, '69. Revised Taylor law is called unduly harsh by Dr. Taylor. Damon Stetson.

New York Times. p 40. Je. 15, '69. Rise of arbitration is seen in disputes of public employees. Damon Stetson.

New York Times. p 1+. Je. 25, '69. Teachers' accord expected to cost 400-million more. Leonard Buder.

New York Times. p 1+. Ag. 2, '69. Mayor urges bargaining office arbitrate city's labor disputes. Martin Tolchin.

*New York Times. p 34. Ag. 11, '69. Less chaos in public service.

New York Times. p 1+. Ag. 28, '69. Group in foreign service seeks to bargain on personnel affairs. Richard Halloran.

New York Times. p 9. S. 19, '69. Germans' strikes impede campaign. Ralph Blumenthal.

New York Times. p 10. O. 2, '69. London garbage strike grows; 16 of 32 boroughs now affected.

New York Times. p 1+. O. 8, '69. Montreal police strike over pay; troops on alert.

New York Times. p 3. O. 8, '69. London garbage strike spreads to other services. J. M. Lee.

New York Times. p 2. O. 9, '69. Clashes erupt in strike of garbagemen in London.

New York Times. p 3. O. 9, '69. Police back in shocked Montreal. Jay Walz.

New York Times. p 5. O. 24, '69. Police in Montreal end wage dispute.

New York Times. p 39. N. 3, '69. Police bar strikes in proposed union. David Burnham.

New York Times Magazine. p 34-5+. F. 25, '68. How to avoid strikes by garbagemen, nurses, teachers, subway men, welfare workers, etc. A. H. Raskin.

New York Times Magazine. p 7-9+. D. 22, '68. Why New York is "strike city." A. H. Raskin.

Notre Dame Lawyer. 43:367-88. F. '68. Teachers' strikes—a new militancy. R. W. Neirynick.

Office. 67:100+. Ja. '68. Union bargaining with public office workers. L. G. Basso.

PTA Magazine. 62:14-15. O. '67. Teacher strikes. W. D. Boutwell.

PTA Magazine. 62:15-16. Je. '68. Dissent in the NEA. W. D. Boutwell.

*Personnel. 46:44-54. Jl.-Ag. '69. Public servants as organized labor. F. P. Zeidler.

Personnel Administration. 30:40-2. Ja. '67. Bargaining-unit relationships in public service. C. Jacobs.

Practical Lawyer. 13:13-22, 79-85. N.-D. '67; 14:83-91. Ja. '68. United States experience in collective bargaining in public employment. Arvid Anderson.

Public Administration Review. 28:111-47. Mr.-Ap. '68. Collective negotiations in the public service: a symposium. F. A. Nigro, ed.

Public Affairs Report. 8:[1-6]. Ag. '67. New militancy of public employees. R. H. Hamilton.
     Same. Good Government 85:3-8. Spring '68; Minnesota Municipalities. 53:124-6+. My. '68.

*Public Interest. p 118-30. Winter '69. Trade unionism goes public. E. M. Kassalow.

Public Management. 48:244+. S. '66. Unions enter city hall: city responsibilities. D. D. Rowlands.

Public Personnel Review. 29:2-6. Ja. '68. Should public employees have the right to strike. R. E. Catlen.

Public Personnel Review. 29:207-11. O. '68. Role of the school superintendent in collective bargaining. E. B. Shils.

Quarterly Review of Economics and Business. 7:29-36. Autumn '67. Public employee strikes: an operational solution. H. L. Fusilier and L. L. Steinmetz.

Reader's Digest. 89:95-9. N. '66. Should teachers strike? Paul Friggens.

*Redbook. 132:67+. Mr. '69. Why teachers are striking. Walter Goodman.

*Saturday Review. 51:27-30+. D. 7, '68. Revolt of the civil servants. A. H. Raskin.

School and Society. 95:226-9. Ap. 1, '67. Professors and collective negotiations. J. F. Day and W. H. Fisher.

School and Society. 96:241-2. Ap. 13, '68. Professional negotiations are not the answer. J. W. Maguire.

Senior Scholastic. 91:14-15. O. 12, '67. Should teachers be allowed to strike? pro and con discussion.

Senior Scholastic. 93:4-7+. D. 13, '68. Public employees and the right to strike; with quotations.

Stanford Law Review. 21:340-82. Ja. '69. Collective bargaining and the California public teacher. Darrell Johnson.

Time. 91:34-5. Mr. 1, '68. Worker's rights and the public weal: Time essay.

*Time. 94:47. O. 17, '69. City without cops.

Today's Education. 57:85-6. S. '68. Teacher opinion poll: should teachers strike?

Today's Education. 58:53-60. Ja. '69. Special feature on professional negotiation: symposium.

UCLA Law Review. 15:840-76. Ap. '68. Teachers, bargaining and strikes: perspective from the Swedish experience. Boyd Hight.

U.S. News & World Report. 60:91-2. Je. 20, '66. It's getting popular to strike against city hall.

U.S. News & World Report. 61:8-9. Ag. 1, '66. Another headache for cities: strikes by public workers.

U.S. News & World Report. 61:96-9. S. 26, '66. Coming: unionized government; interview. Jerry Wurf.

U.S. News & World Report. 63:74-5. Ag. 14, '67. If 100,000 teachers go on strike.

U.S. News & World Report. 64:84-5. F. 19, '68. Why teachers strike: too little pay, too much work.

U.S. News & World Report. 64:78-9. F. 26, '68. Militant public employees: more trouble for the cities.

U.S. News & World Report. 65:41-2. S. 2, '68. Coming rash of teacher strikes.

U.S. News & World Report. 65:83-4. S. 16, '68. Teachers on strike: what they want now.

*U.S. News & World Report. 65:62-3. D. 30, '68. What other countries do about strikes against public.

U.S. News & World Report. 66:37-9. Mr. 3, '69. One reason your taxes keep going higher and higher.

*Wall Street Journal. 170:8. S. 15, '67. What rights has a public employee? Jerry Wurf.
        Same. Good Government. 85:20-2. Spring '68.

Wall Street Journal. 171:1+. Je. 3, '68. Union on the move [AFSCME]. R. J. Levine.

Wall Street Journal. 172:1+. Ag. 20, '68. Militant teachers. R. J. Levine.

Wall Street Journal. 172:1+. S. 9, '68. Delaying the mail? Restive postal workers pose mounting threat of wildcat walkouts. R. J. Levine.

Wall Street Journal. 172:20. S. 10, '68. Different point of view [editorial].
Wall Street Journal. 172:1+. O. 18, '68. Unionists under fire (post office employees). J. P. Gannon.
Wall Street Journal. 173:14. My. 12, '69. Blount favors "true" joint bargaining for postal employees.
*Wilson Library Bulletin. 43:752-5. Ap. '69. Unions—what's in it for administrators? Darryl Mleynek.